Solving the

WEST GEORGIA
MURDER
OF
Gwendolyn Moore

A CRY FROM
THE WELL

CLAY BRYANT

THE
History
PRESS

Published by The History Press
Charleston, SC
www.historypress.com

First published 2021

Manufactured in the United States

ISBN 9781467150071

Library of Congress Control Number: 2021937190

Notice: The information in this book is true and complete to the best of our knowledge. It is offered without guarantee on the part of the author or The History Press. The author and The History Press disclaim all liability in connection with the use of this book.

CONTENTS

Contents

PREFACE

A deeply rooted southern tradition, friendly yet intense competition, quiet camaraderie and restrained excitement—all are integral elements of the gentleman's sport of night hunting. What began as a contest between neighbors became a cottage industry, with serious hunters paying literally tens of thousands of dollars for the best of hounds to ensure success.

The familiarity and bond between a hunter and his dog make this sport unlike any other. These competitions serve as a show of not only whose dog is the best but also which hunter knows and understands his hound the most. When a hound "strikes the trail" or catches the scent of the raccoon, points are awarded in order by the cast judge—from one hundred for the first dog to strike down to twenty-five points for the last of four hounds to strike.

The catch is that if a hunter strikes his dog first, the hound has to run that track to a conclusion and tree a coon. At the tree, the dog's voice will change, and the hunter will know when his dog hits the tree. As with the strikes, a hound is awarded points for treeing. The hunter has to be confident that his dog has circled the tree and made sure that the coon has not climbed out on a limb and jumped down, leaving the dog at a false tree. If the coon can't be found, then all points awarded become negative in the same succession as they were awarded. If a dog isn't rock solid, he has little chance of placing well in the hunt.

A hunter has to know his dog. He must understand what the dog is telling him, have faith in the ability of his hound and be able to call what the dog tells him. My father could identify the voice of each dog and explain in detail what that voice was telling him—a sacred ritual that has been repeated through the generations.

As the events of a hunt unfolded, I watched many times my father leaning on the dog box in the bed of our old Ford pickup. As he listened to the music of the chase, he would be twiddling his thumbs with that boyish grin flashing across his face. As he became sure of the voice of his hound, he would turn to the cast judge with pride and surety and proclaim, "You can strike my dog." It was with that same love and understanding he would say to me growing up, "Son, you're my dog if you never strike a track."

In my career as an investigator, I've tried to deserve that trust. What follows is the story of Gwendolyn Moore, a defenseless woman denied mercy in her life and justice after her murder, as well as my determination to bring the truth to light.

ACKNOWLEDGEMENTS

I would like to give special thanks to all those who have contributed to this book, for without their help and support, there would have been no book. There also would have been no justice for Gwendolyn.

For going above and beyond in the search for thirty-three-year-old records that no one thought could be found, I thank Diane Ennis, Dawn Pierce and Chris Hosey with the Georgia Bureau of Investigation.

I thank Kaye Minchew, Barry Jackson, Lance Jones and Diana Thompson of the Troup County Archives.

I thank Dr. Kris Sperry (pathologist) and Dr. Rick Snow (criminal anthropologist), of the Georgia Bureau of Investigation, to whom Gwen told her story. I thank Agent Gary Fuller (Ret.), of the Georgia Bureau of Investigation, for his time and assistance when he could have been fishing.

Patty Smith and Jeanie Henderson, with the Troup County District Attorney's Office, spent hours of transcription as volunteers.

Lysette Strickland (GBI Crime Lab) and the McKibben Funeral Home of Hogansville, Georgia, helped see that Gwendolyn made it home.

Pete Skandalakis, director of the Georgia Prosecuting Attorney's Council, gave me the opportunity to make a difference in the lives of victims and families like that of Gwendolyn Moore and others to come.

Jackie Kennedy and Elizabeth Sullivan helped me with editing and inspiration.

I thank my wife, Beth, and the kids to make up for the times when you were ignored while my mind was on this.

ACKNOWLEDGEMENTS

To professor John Williams, without your help and direction, my dream of publishing this book would not have come true.

I thank my daddy, Buddy Bryant, for teaching me that truth, accountability and justice mean something.

THANK YOU AND MAY GOD BLESS YOU ALL!

PROLOGUE

S ome memories never fade. The intensity of the images and recollections brings to the surface a kick-in-the-gut physical response that can be felt in the core of your being. On the December afternoon Allen Moore spoke of the last time he saw his mother alive, I was acutely aware that the shiver running down my spine was not from the cold winter air. I listened intently as Allen, choking back tears, recounted the horrendous story of family violence that had haunted him for well over thirty years. The pain he still felt and the impact of the brutality he witnessed had on his life were apparent in every word he spoke. He was a far cry from the young boy I had grown up knowing in a small Georgia town, and our separate worlds were about to be joined in a way I never could have imagined. We were raised a mere stone's throw from each other, but the reality of our lives was truly worlds apart.

For the first time in thirty-two years, Moore could verbalize the events of that fateful, hot August night in 1970. His anguish was apparent in the tremors and anger in his voice as he relived the darkest day of his young life, as he unburdened himself of the misplaced guilt he had carried all these years.

Allen and I were young men being raised on opposite sides of town in Hogansville, Georgia, a dot on the map in west-central Georgia. As the son of the local police chief, I was raised by generous and loving parents who nurtured and encouraged me. Allen Moore grew up in fear, witnessing the torturous life, and then death, of the only loving person in his life.

I knew Allen back then, but I never could have imagined at my tender and somewhat sheltered age of fifteen what he had seen and suffered through. And now, here we were, more than three decades later, and I was finally getting to know Allen Moore—it was about thirty-two years too late. As he described the details of that dreadful day in 1970, I pulled forth my own recollection of that horrific time.

Tuesday, August 4, 1970, found me, as most days did, trailing behind my daddy. A decent and justice-seeking man, well loved by his community, L.G. "Buddy" Bryant was known as an innovator in law enforcement at a time when most small-town police officers were known only for the zeal with which they approached their jobs. I loved and admired him and hoped to follow in his footsteps one day. So, when on that morning my daddy hung up the phone and said to me, "Clay-boy, ride out to Junior Turner's with me. The Sheriff's Office wants us to stand by until they arrive. They've got a body in the old well next to Junior's, and they want me to take some photographs for them," I was ready. On the drive out Mobley Bridge Road, Daddy called for a wrecker to respond to the scene to help with the recovery.

Junior Turner lived on the corner of Lee Street and Mobley Bridge Road, the first house outside the city limits of Hogansville in unincorporated Troup County, a geographical fact that ultimately would forestall justice for what seemed like an eternity to Allen Moore.

A crowd had gathered just across South Lee Street at the old house site adjacent to Junior's yard. The group stood in the overgrowth of what was once a lawn, and we could hear murmurs of curiosity tinged with morbid fascination. The crowd moved as one, restlessly, until stilled by the collection of arriving officials. As did most old houses of the time, this one had a well curbed to the side of the porch before the old house burned down. There was no longer a rod-and-pulley system to the old hand-dug well with which to draw water, but rather an open hole that the neighbors had been using as a garbage dump. After surveying the situation, my father immediately began to give instructions to launch the recovery of the body. Not having been told not to, I peered wide-eyed into the dry well, which had an opening about five feet across. I could see a woman's body some twenty-five feet or so down at the bottom of the dry well—in a crouched position, as though she were praying.

All the particulars of that day at the well are not sharp in my mind, but two things remain burned into my memory: Allen and his little brother Ricky, standing off to the side crying, as well as the surreal image of that poor soul twisting on the end of the wrecker's cable after being pulled up from the depths of the well, her body suspended over that hellish garbage-strewn pit, her blouse splattered with blood and her eyes swollen shut. Dried blood, a deep maroon color, covered her face, and her entire body was mottled black and blue.

The silence was shattered by members of the crowd voicing their thoughts: "He finally did it"…"I don't see how she stood it as long as she did." The neighbors spoke in hushed tones, whispers that would become screams for justice at a much later date.

Without ceremony, the body was loaded into the McKibben Funeral Home hearse, and slowly, the dismayed crowd began to disperse. As we drove away, my dad said the words that would come back to me full force: "I feel ashamed that I couldn't do something for that poor woman." My daddy knew things about the situation that I did not, details that I would have no knowledge of for many years to come. On that miserable day in 1970, he told me that it should not have come to this for something to be done. He felt convinced that from what he knew, this was not a tragic accident—the woman had been killed and thrown down the well.

As we drove away, I felt sure that the mystery of the death of Gwendolyn Moore would be solved and that the man my daddy believed was her killer, her husband, Marshall, would be brought to justice. As we headed farther down the road, my thoughts turned to Allen and the other boys, Ricky and Larry, and the baby of six months, Dean. What would become of them?

THE SNAKES CRAWL UP THE RIVER

To fully understand the cultural, political and social climate in 1970 Troup County, Georgia, one needs to know a little of the regional history. In order to do this, you have to begin by looking a little farther down the river and across the Alabama state line.

John Will and Lou Shepherd raised their family of five sons and five daughters between homes in Randolph County, Alabama, and LaGrange, Georgia, during the late 1800s and early 1900s. Natives of Randolph County, they moved their family to LaGrange in 1912. Of the five sons, Robert Loren died during the flu epidemic of 1918 at the age of eleven. Wallace Shepherd remained in LaGrange and became a successful businessman. The other three brothers—Hoyt, Grady and Roy—all went south and made Phenix City, Alabama, their home.

Seeing the proximity of Fort Benning, with its limitless number of young men to be preyed on, Hoyt Shepherd became an entrepreneur dealing in nearly every vice to be had at the time.

Nestled along the banks of the Chattahoochee River and lying directly across from the bustling army town of Columbus, Georgia, stood a den of iniquity known as Phenix City, Alabama. The dismal history of Phenix City (and Russell County, Alabama) is well documented, as the city gained infamy throughout the country for its reputation as a lair of crime and corruption. At one time, General George Patton threatened to lay siege to the city and take his Third Army across the Chattahoochee River Bridge from Columbus into Phenix City. Patton considered seriously the detrimental effect the vices of the town were having on soldiers training at Fort Benning in preparation for their entry into World War II. Scattered throughout the city were bars, gambling houses and brothels, all of which were readily available; the purveyors of sin were eager to lure in the next victim. More than once, fledgling soldiers were found floating in the Chattahoochee after being rolled for their small wages by the scoundrels of Phenix City. The inexperienced young men became tragic victims of what was known at the time as the most corrupt city in the country, as noted by an exposé published in the early 1940s in *TIME* magazine. The army's response was to declare Phenix City once and for all off-limits to all military personnel.

The city was run by what would later become known as the "Old Dixie Mafia," headed by Hoyt Shepherd and his partner, Jimmy Mathews. Together they owned and operated the Bama Club, the largest and most notorious of all the many illegal clubs in Phenix City. It offered all types of gambling, cards, roulette and horse racing, as well as prostitution and illegal liquor. The Bama Club drew clientele from all over the country. Hoyt was a big man—big in respect to his gut, his ego and his meanness. He was protected by his cohort and partner in crime, Sheriff Ralph Matthews, an intelligent and ruthless man yet engaging and charming in an Al Capone kind of way. These men were the backbone of the Mafia and controlled their domain with an iron fist. In September 1946, Hoyt; his brother Grady "Snooks" Shepherd; and business partner, Jimmy Mathews, were charged with the murder of rival club owner Fate Leebern.

Leebern owned the Southern Manor, where the killing took place. At trial, Grady Shepherd confessed to killing Leebern but claimed self-defense. Hoyt Shepherd and Jimmy Mathews were acquitted of the murder. The defense team for the trio was headed up by a young and up-and-coming attorney named Vernon Belcher, a name that would arise again years later a little farther upstream on the Chattahoochee. The members of the Mafia were ruthless and exceedingly violent in their pursuit of the seemingly endless supply of money their criminal enterprises produced. In addition to controlling the liquor, gambling and prostitution rings, the Dixie Mafia had a strong hand in local government as well.

The situation became so outrageous that in 1953, Albert Patterson, a respected war veteran and Phenix City lawyer, ran for attorney general of Alabama on the platform that he would clean up Phenix City. Patterson had actually defended Hoyt Shepherd at trial for a murder of which he was acquitted shortly after Patterson returned from the war. It did not take

Patterson long to realize the true situation in Phenix City; being a man of conscience, he felt compelled to seek a position that would allow him to rid the community of its national criminal reputation. Although there were multiple, widespread attempts to steal the election from him, Patterson won the people's vote and was elected to the position. In a speech to his supporters after being elected, Albert Patterson prophetically proclaimed that he felt there was one chance in one hundred that he would ever be sworn in as Alabama's attorney general.

The Dixie Mafia's answer to this attempt to end its unscrupulous domination? On June 18, 1954, Mr. Patterson was shot and killed in broad daylight as he left his law office in downtown Phenix City; of course, the investigation, led by Sheriff Matthews, could find no witnesses or evidence of who Patterson's killer may have been.

One needs to understand that tentacles of corruption of this magnitude ran far and deep, in this case all the way to the state capital in Montgomery. The Phenix City Crew (headed by Hoyt Shepherd and his partner Jimmy Mathews, later known as the "Old Dixie Mafia") had found a friend in Attorney General Si Garrett, who, being the state's highest-ranking law enforcement officer, had become complicit with the crime bosses of Phenix City. However, in early 1954, the winds of change had become strong enough to demand action, and Sheriff Mathews was removed from office; the investigation into Albert Patterson's assassination was revived, and witnesses and evidence were developed that led to the indictments of Attorney General Si Garrett, Russell County solicitor Arch Ferrell and the trigger man, Sheriff Matthew's chief deputy, Albert Fuller. Fuller was convicted of the murder and was sentenced to life in prison. Garrett, who claimed a defense of insanity, was deemed mentally incompetent to stand trial after examination by a state mental health psychologist, and Ferrell was eventually acquitted.

Public outcry over this deplorable turn of events prompted the then governor of Alabama, Gordon Parsons, to declare a state of martial law in Phenix City and Russell County. Parsons ordered General Walter J. Hanna, commanding officer of the Alabama National Guard, to gather his troops and travel immediately to Phenix City in order to relieve all law enforcement officials in the city of their duties until an interim government could be installed. General Hanna and his men rounded up all those involved in the rackets of Phenix City, and ultimately, a blue ribbon grand jury was empaneled to investigate the corruption. The grand jury eventually handed down 545 indictments on fifty-nine different defendants, with the indictments ranging from murder to willful neglect of duty by the law enforcement officials of Phenix City for their complicity in the rackets.

Sheriff Ralph Matthews was indicted on September 3, 1954, for willful neglect of his duties, and he pleaded guilty to the charge on December 9, 1954. Thus began a new era in Phenix City. After the cleanup of 1954, Phenix City prospered and evolved into a clean and respectable community.

In direct conjunction with Phenix City making its transition from criminality to propriety, the influence of the ol' boys from down the Chattahoochee traveled upstream to set up shop in LaGrange, Georgia, and Troup County.

Wallace Shepherd had a son, Robert, who had drawn close to his uncle Hoyt. Robert worked for his father in his legitimate businesses. According to family sources, Robert had an obsession with criminality; he would sit and watch crime shows like *The Untouchables* for hours on end. Robert admired Uncle Hoyt's lifestyle as a gangster and crime boss. It was Hoyt's influence that led to Robert opening his own criminal enterprise, the Eagles Club. It provided illegal gambling with craps and card tables, as well as slot machines. He would soon branch out to provide all the other clubs in the area with liquor and the tools necessary to satisfy the tastes of all those who sought these vices.

It was one of those situations that was both loved and feared by the community, where everyone knew about, but no one spoke of, the gentlemen's true purpose. Troup County was a dry county, but there were "private clubs" that had always been in existence. These clubs sold liquor and provided a safe haven for gambling and the like. For the most part, the community tolerated these sites because they were low-key establishments and provided the necessary evils.

In organizations such as the Moose Club, the Elks Club, the American Legion, the Veterans of Foreign Wars, the Eagles Club and others, alcohol could not be wholesaled—it had to be bootlegged. The Boys stepped right in to fill this bill. In little time, they managed the vices of Troup County as completely and lucratively as they had farther down the river. The downstream influence and the Shepherd clan had quickly stepped in and taken charge in an uncharacteristically quiet manner.

J. Ralph Matthews and the Boys rapidly infiltrated the Troup County Democratic Committee; this provided political protection for "the Machine." In doing so, they commandeered Sheriff Lem Bailey into the fold. Sheriff Bailey was the consummate politician; he remembered the names of every person and their children in Troup County. As good as

Robert Shepherd, drunk on a horse, circa 1962. *Del Kuhlman Private Collection.*

Sheriff Bailey was as a politician, he was just as poor as a lawman. When it came to problems with the law, Ralph Mathews, through his "pal" and cohort Lem Bailey, could get you out of just about any mess you could get yourself into—considering, of course, the amount of money you were willing to spend and what status in society you held. Old Lem had an affinity for the ladies and liquor, an Achilles' heel that would keep him squarely in the Boys' pockets for the rest of his tenure.

Lem Bailey was an angular man, tall and thin. His sharp face was adorned with the tell-tale flushed cheeks and mottled nose of one who drank in excess. As a boy, I remember being at suppers and community events with Sheriff Bailey, who often appeared to be six sheets to the wind. Lem always wore a fedora hat, and when he was drinking, he had a habit of rolling his shoulders and making a sucking noise through his teeth as he drew on his cigarette. His unassuming appearance belied his power and the unscrupulous nature of his character.

J. Ralph Matthews owned Troup Bonding and Loan Company and Matthews Real Estate, which were located in the Matthews Building on Hill Street in the Three Points neighborhood of LaGrange. The building itself

Members of the Troup County Sheriff's Department. *First row, from left to right*: Sheriff L.W. Lem Bailey, Secretary Joyce Bryan and Chief Deputy Mack Smith. *Second row, from left to right*: Deputy Harry Floyd, jailer Bill "Ump" Hood and Deputy Jerry Bryan. *Third row, from left to right*: jailer Al Willis, Deputy Billy East, Deputy Johnny McCurry and Deputy Boots Aiken. Circa 1965. *Del Kuhlman Private Collection.*

was large and imposing white brick and at one time housed both a dance hall and a radio station. Matthews's office was in the back of the building and was fronted by a workforce that included bondsmen/bounty hunters as well as secretaries. Both of his businesses were run with direct assistance from the Troup County Sheriff's Office. On any given Friday or Saturday night, you could walk through the entrance of the county jail and a Troup Bonding Company agent would be on duty at a table just past the jailer. On the table would be a stack of security bonds and a stack of personal loan notes from the loan company. Anyone who was arrested by the deputies or the state patrol was offered the services of the bonding agent. Unless you were recognized as one of the county's elite or you happened to have a deed to some real estate in your pocket at the time of your arrest that could be approved by the sheriff, your choices became jail time or having to avail yourself of the bondsman lying in wait.

The bondsman not only charged you a percentage to sign the bond, but he also had you sign a loan note for the full amount of the bond. Some sort of collateral would be created for the note, and the arrested party would be released on a promise to pay the bonding fee. If the fee were not paid in a manner deemed timely by the bondsman, the Sheriff's Office would issue a warrant for endangering a security interest for not producing the recorded collateral. The defendant would then be re-arrested and put in jail; after a day or two of the defendant cooling his heels in Sheriff Bailey's pokey, a bond would be set and the process would be repeated.

The system tirelessly fed on the poor and uneducated. Bonds were signed with no risk and a jailhouse guarantee of their fee. If by some slim chance a defendant did jump bond and the bonding company was at risk, the sheriff simply used his influence to have the case dismissed. No case, no bond liability.

The Shepherds had their hands on other throttles of the Machine: illegal liquor, commercial gambling, influence and protection. One of Robert Shepherd's daughters told me that when there was going to be a cosmetic vice raid on one of the local clubs that had slot machines, "Lem would call Daddy and he would bring the one armed bandits home in a U-Haul, and he'd give us quarters to play them in the truck until he could take them back to the club." The corrupt political machine roared through Troup County in the 1960s and '70s. Ralph's control on local politics was unprecedented. Even though he was never completely socially accepted by the Troup County old money elite, he wielded more political influence than anyone in West Georgia. With him or one of his minions holding the chair of the Troup County Democratic Committee, Ralph was able to broker power and influence right into the front door of the state capitol. When a man needed help with a "problem" concerning the state government, help was no farther away than a visit to J. Ralph Matthews: jobs with any state agency; assistance with influence at any state agency, such as getting a prisoner transferred from one prison to another; or getting a driveway installed from a state highway onto your property.

Ralph was probably one of only a few from Troup County who could call the governor on a private line that the governor would answer directly. The governor always lent J. Ralph a listening ear, for he was in position to control and broker support for the chosen Democratic candidates. During those days, unlike today, the Republican Party in the South was a non-issue.

Ralph would use this influence with the governor to help secure a judgeship appointment to the Troup County State Court for Vernon Belcher of Phenix City fame. It was Vernon Belcher who had defended Jimmy Mathews and the Shepherd brothers for the murder of Fate Leebern. With Troup County's law enforcement and the State Court Judiciary under their thumb, the Boys had control of Troup County's system of injustice. The Superior Court, however, was another matter. Judge J.C. Jackson was not for sale, and he would usually position himself as far away from the Machine as he possibly could. But with what they had, the Boys just worked around the Superior Court and continued to deal in all the necessary vices to keep the wheels turning with money and influence.

When it came to the Boys and their Machine, Sheriff Bailey was at their beck and call. He had a lucrative position as the front man for the Machine, and he wasn't about to jeopardize it by crossing swords with the powers that be over what he felt was an unfortunate but insignificant occurrence, such as the loss of a poor country girl dealt a bad lot in life.

My father, L.G. ("Buddy") Bryant, summarized the source of the political machine that controlled Troup County from the late 1950s until 1980 in his usual vivid yet jovial manner: "When the governor of Alabama saw fit to drain the swamp known as Phenix City, some of the snakes slipped up the river and crawled out on the banks of Troup County."

Unfortunately, because of the state of affairs in the county, the memory of Gwendolyn Moore would be forgotten by all but a very few. Soon her cries from the well would fall deathly silent.

The Law According to Buddy

S on, the world is full of policemen, but there are very few peace officers. If this is what you want to do, for God's sake, be a peace officer." Those were the words of wisdom imparted by the best peace officer I have ever known, my father. Not only was Buddy Bryant a wise, kind and generous man, but above all else his sense of fairness was also apparent in every task or case he undertook.

To say I was in awe of my father is an understatement. As I grew into manhood, I watched with pride as he operated with the wisdom of Solomon and the patience of Job. I admired my father most certainly, but I also considered him to be my best friend, an assertion I believe few men can make claim to in their own relationships with their fathers. Buddy had a gift: an ability to soothe the savage beast of sorts. He would respond to a fight between two neighbors who were cussing and brawling in the yard, and by the time Buddy was done talking, everybody involved in the altercation would be sitting at a table sharing supper, each one thinking smugly to himself that he had won the argument. Yes, indeed, Buddy had the magic touch.

This is not to imply that my daddy was without his faults. He served as Hogansville's chief of police for twenty-two years, an implausibly long term for a small town. This feat was even more incredible considering the fact that my father was an alcoholic. As a binge drinker, he might go a year and never touch a drop, but when Buddy decided he could handle a drink, it was just a matter of time before he would become incapacitated for days on end. Buddy was not violent or loud when he was in the bottle; he would

Chief Buddy Bryant, circa 1975. *Author's collection.*

just go into his own shell at home and drink until he ran out, but sometimes that could take a while.

Because Daddy and I were best friends, his opinion of my actions and decisions in life meant the world to me. If I had done something he considered not up to par, he never laid a hand on me as punishment, but the look he could give that showed his disappointment in something I had done could crush me to my soul. There was nothing in the world we didn't talk about, and his demons, products of his childhood, were no exception.

Jim and Alma Bryant raised Buddy, their eldest boy, in Grantville, Georgia. Vivian, the eldest daughter; James (or Uncle LaVerne, as I knew him), the second son; and baby brother Chester rounded out the family. Jim Bryant worked hard in the Banks Cotton Mill most of his life, with an occasional venture into businesses such as a small hardware store and, later in life, the flower and plant business.

Times were never easy for the Bryant family. The two eldest boys worked hard at outside jobs or on the family farm. Jim ruled with an iron fist during the boys' younger years, and any variance from the rules was dealt with quickly and harshly. As a result, Buddy grew closer to his mother, who also had to deal with Jim's ill temper. It was just a matter of time before the children grew old enough to move away from the tension and fear. Uncle LaVerne left first, moving to Texas to live with relatives. He told me years later that he made the move to keep his father from killing him…or him from killing his father.

Daddy left a year later when he joined the service. Buddy would tell me that he just couldn't understand how Jim could be so kind to everyone else and so harsh with his own family. After Daddy was grown, he and his father came to a peace and became close, but Buddy could never completely separate himself from those painful memories of his past. They fueled a fire that, from time to time, would send him down a road bent on self-destruction.

I'm not sure what provoked a complete turnaround in Jim's nature in his later years. It may have been the thought of losing his sons who, over time, had put ample distance between themselves and their father. Perhaps it was the guilt of coming to grips with mistreating the ones he loved. But for

Buddy and Clay, 1978.
Author's collection.

whatever reason, by the time I got old enough to remember Jim—or Papa, as I called him—he had become much more mellow and relaxed. He was always kind to me and seemed to enjoy the countless hours we spent together hunting and fishing. On occasion, he would tell me how he had put away the foolishness he suffered as a young man—that he had done things in his life he wished he could do over. He never said exactly what those things were, but I understood. I never heard him say a bad or condemning word about any person, living or dead.

I can honestly say that Papa evolved into one of the most decent human beings I had ever known. Although he might have been lacking as a father to Buddy, he made a great grandfather to me. Papa must have been a better father than Daddy thought as far as passing along some important life lessons, though, because Buddy seemed to have learned a great deal about the world and people from somewhere. Daddy always said that the mark of an intelligent man is not in the fact that he made no mistakes, but rather in what he was able to learn from his mistakes. He took that even a little further, adding that a good man used what he learned to become a better man. Papa was indeed a good and intelligent man, and my life was made richer for it.

One of the many things my daddy taught me was that a man has to learn to accept people for who and what they are—even in the best of men, there are some bad traits, and in many cases, there are some good traits in the worst of men. Tolerance, he would say, is the key to dealing with the shortcomings of people; this was the maxim by which he lived. Sometimes I would ask him why he tolerated some people whose characters I know he didn't respect or care for. "Son," he would say, "you always keep a snake where you can see him, and he won't be able to bite you." Buddy, however, could not abide a man taking advantage of those who could not defend themselves, particularly women, children, old people and those who were simple-minded. "There's a special hot place in Hell for any man that mistreats them," he would declare.

Most people loved Buddy, shortcomings and all. I can't count the number of people who have come up to me throughout the course of my lifetime and said, "Your daddy helped me"…"Your daddy did something for my family"…"Your daddy sent me to the chain gang, but he wouldn't have done it if I hadn't needed to go. He probably saved my life."

I don't know if he brainwashed me along the way, but my main mission in life was to please my dad. In much the same way as he was hell-bent on being close to me, in response to his own childhood relationship with Jim, I made it my mission not to repeat the actions I saw as flaws in my daddy's character. For that reason, I never drank or smoked while I was growing up. I knew that my daddy didn't want me to fall into the same snares that had entangled him.

When it came to law enforcement, Buddy was recognized as somewhat of an aberration. In the 1950s and '60s, education was not exactly held at a premium in police circles. The rule of thumb was the bigger the nightstick, the more effective the policeman. A bit of an innovator, Buddy foresaw the winds of change. He graduated from the first class of the Georgia State Police Academy in 1966. He attended the Southern Police Institute in Louisville, Kentucky, and was an FBI-certified fingerprint expert, one of only half a dozen in the state at that time. Lord only knows the professional seminars and training programs he attended. His unquenchable thirst for knowledge eventually elevated him to the status of chief of police in a profession he loved dearly.

Buddy and Clay Bryant, circa 1964. *Author's collection.*

Whether it was intuition, instinct or some type of sixth sense, when it came to solving crimes, Buddy had it. Be it a stolen bicycle or a murder, he would collect the evidence, go sit at the radio desk at the police department and stare at the old Motorola microphone sitting on the desktop. He would settle back into his chair, twiddle his thumbs and ruminate, all the while formulating his plan of action. After some time, he would stand up and say, "Let's go." Inevitably, following a few stops around the neighborhood to talk with informants, someone would end up sitting at his desk writing out their confession.

Buddy always said, "Any officer who doesn't know his community and have its support needs to find himself another line of work because he will never be effective." Daddy also once told me, "Son, the ruination of policing was the day they put air conditioning in a patrol car. On that day, it became comfortable for an officer to isolate himself from the people he serves." I grew to understand that the bond he built and enjoyed with his community was what made him so successful. He knew the good, the bad and everyone in between, and he made it his business to know all the local criminals, their tendencies and quirks. He purposely and diligently stayed in touch with the neighborhood miscreants. "I know and love everybody in every church pew in Hogansville, Georgia, but if they were the only people that liked and

Members of the Hogansville Police Department, 1967. *From left to right*: Buddy Bryant, H.T. Horton, Lee Walker, Charlie Frank Green, Marshall Cardwell, C.E. Baker, L.M. ("Dick") Staley and Gene Talley. *Author's collection.*

trusted me enough to tell me the things I need to know, I'd be a worthless lawman," Buddy would remark.

When an offense occurred, he already had in his mind a list of suspects as soon as he walked onto the crime scene. To my daddy, an investigator's worst enemy was a closed mind because sometimes you could let that stand between you and the truth. In his twenty years as chief, his crowning achievement was that he never once lost a case as prosecutor in Superior Court. His motto was "If you've got a case, work it until it's a good case; and if you don't have a case, don't insult the court and yourself by bringing it to the bar." Many officers today would benefit from that nugget of wisdom.

Buddy always made time for folks. It didn't matter if it was the president of the bank at 1:30 p.m. on a Tuesday afternoon or one of the town drunks banging on the door of our house at 7:00 a.m. on Sunday morning— everyone got to voice his or her problem. And Buddy would always follow through with doing whatever he committed to doing for them. A man with no money or influence was no less a man, my father believed, and so he treated them all with equal respect. His philosophy in life and in work was that the little problems of others were not insignificant to them, and a true peace officer would always do what he would expect to be done for him.

If you operated under this golden rule of service, you would always do the fair thing, my daddy said. He was a peace officer of the highest caliber, and as important as that was, I believe his greatest success in life was his role as a father.

In 1970 Troup County, however, not all police officers shared Buddy's affection for justice. "It's a shame that what should be fair for all is so partial to the few in the county," Daddy said one day as he gazed out the kitchen window of our home. He had just heard that the Gwendolyn Moore case, which had held his interest so closely for the past two months, was for all intents and purposes closed. "How could he have not done it? There was enough evidence to convict the Pope," Buddy lamented. "If it had just been across the road in the city limits, he'd be on his way to death row in Tattnall County right this minute. But that sheriff's going to let him go." With sorrow in his eyes and a burden on his heart because of the jurisdictional lines that would not allow him to become involved in the case, he whispered in anguish, "One day I'll be in a position to set the record straight."

It seemed obvious to my daddy that Troup County sheriff Lem Bailey had no interest in the particulars of the case or the results of the investigation. But Daddy knew as well as anyone that even though Bailey was the head law enforcement officer in the county and the captain of the ship, he was not the one who charted its course. To the powers that ran the Machine that controlled justice in Troup County, this case and the lives it would affect meant nothing—it would not even cause a bump in the road as the Machine rolled along.

"The law's highest function is to protect the rights of all the people, especially those who can't protect themselves," Buddy told me time and time again. "The greatest reward a peace officer can have is the satisfaction of knowing he has done something to protect the helpless."

My daddy loved that part of his job. That is why the memory of Gwendolyn Moore haunted him so. He could hear her frightened voice from the bottom of the well—lonesome, forsaken and pleading for justice.

Allen's Road

H e killed my mama and put her in the well, and if he finds out I'm telling you this, he'll kill me too."

Just over a week had passed since fourteen-year-old Allen Moore stood at the side of the well, quivering in fear and apprehension, horrified at the sight of his mother's battered body. Now he sat trembling yet stoic in front of Agent Troy Owen of the Georgia Bureau of Investigation (GBI), the man Sheriff Lem Bailey had enlisted to lead the probe into the death of Gwendolyn Moore.

At this time, the GBI was not the elite crime fighting organization of today. In 1970, GBI agents were assigned counties, and they worked "at the pleasure of the sheriff." This investigative discretion allowed an opportunity for the sheriff to dispose of cases for political reasons whenever he felt the need to do so. The Troup County sheriff wanted no part of justice for Gwendolyn. As far as he was concerned, the investigation would create more problems for him in areas he couldn't afford. Sheriff Bailey now had the perfect response to the neighbors and others outraged by the situation: the GBI was handling the case, and it was out of his hands. He had not only his scapegoat but also total control of the outcome.

Allen was left more alone than he had ever been. In a life dominated by brutality and cruelty at the hands of his own father, he had just lost the only person in the world who could insulate him from this misery. For Marshall Moore's callous indifference and savagery did not stop at his diminutive wife—the children were also targets of countless beatings. Whenever his smoldering rage surfaced, no victim was spared. Gwendolyn had always assumed the role of protector, placing herself in harm's way to shield her beloved children. And now she was gone.

Caught in a terrifying catch-22, Allen was in the impossible position of knowing the truth of what had happened to his mother while having to live with the man responsible for her death. Worse, he would now be the one to inherit the primary role of victim as his father vented his uncontrollable anger.

Perhaps the greatest injustice was the guilt Allen bore for his mother's death. He could not reconcile within his impressionable mind that he was just as much a victim, having been witness to the abuse for the whole of his entire life. No one could imagine the horrors this young man had observed and undergone in his tortured fourteen years of childhood.

Allen's life was filled with many such memories, but one in particular stood out. In 1966, the family lived in DeKalb County on Henrico Road. One day, Allen and his baby brother Ricky had been told by their father to wait in the car outside the house. Ricky was playing with the blinker handle in the car and broke it. Allen knew what was about to take place—he had been filled with dread many times before as he waited for the inescapable savagery to unfold. Aware that his father's reaction would surely result in a severe beating of little Ricky at best, he felt he could handle the results of his father's rage better. As his mother had done so many times before, Allen stepped in to take the brunt of his father's barbarity. He confessed that he had broken the signal lever, knowing full well the consequences.

Marshall Moore's alcohol-fueled rages were consistent and unsparing. He stormed off the front porch of the house and grabbed a swing chain, a device made of cut and twisted steel wire, barbed at the links where they were joined—a tool of torture that one would associate with a macabre story of horror. To Marshall Moore, it was a sadistic device to inflict his brand of inhumanity on his own child. Allen remembered only his father lifting him up by the arm and the searing pain of the first few blows as the chain tore paths across his back. Mercifully, Allen was spared the memory of the rest of the beating, as he was rendered unconscious. His sole recollection is waking up and being stuck to the bed by the dried blood from his wounds.

Allen Moore, 1971, from the Hogansville High yearbook. *Author's collection.*

As the wounded boy lay crying and afraid, his body ravaged by his father's hand, he heard footsteps coming into the room and the quiet voice of his mother trying not to be overheard by his assaulter. She wiped his tears first, and then her own, as she used the warm, damp washcloth to soften the blood that had him glued to the sheets. In quiet whispers, Gwendolyn tried to comfort her son and reassure him that things would be all right.

Piercing the sorrowful quiet, Marshall Moore's voice erupted, "Just what in the hell do you think you are doing? If I had wanted him petted, I'd done it myself. I'm sick of you going behind my back with these young'uns," he slurred, his muscular frame looming in the doorway. Allen cowered in the corner as Marshall grabbed Gwendolyn by the hair and, with a crashing blow of his massive hand, sent her reeling to the floor. He swaggered over to her like a hunter approaching his kill. Still pumped up on adrenaline from his exertion, he reached down and tore her clothes away. Marshall liked to see the results of his handiwork. Gwendolyn's eye was already swelling shut, and he reached down to pull her up by her hair; again he slammed her to the floor with another powerful blow to the head.

As always, Allen wished he could save his mother from the vicious beating she took over the next several minutes, which seemed like years as Allen listened and watched in fear. After Marshall's rage subsided, he left Allen and Gwendolyn alone in the room. Allen moved to his mother's side. He thought she was dead and wished it had been he who had been the recipient of his father's fury.

Gwendolyn remained hospitalized and unconscious for three days following that assault. She recovered, but she was told that she could not continue taking these beatings to the head without suffering severe long-term damage. Allen was relieved to have his protector still alive, but he continued to feel guilty for what was happening to his mother.

Allen would continue to witness this same type of violence over the next four years, just as he had since he was old enough to remember. Even though he felt powerless to bring to a halt the repeated attacks, he felt unceasing shame for not being able to stop the inhumanity against Gwendolyn. A boy wants to be a man, but up against a beast like his father, how much of a man could a fourteen-year-old child be? There was no way the young boy could have known the truth: the beatings weren't because Gwendolyn and the boys were bad people—they weren't bad at all. They were good people. It wasn't about Gwendolyn or the kids. It was about power and control and the rush Marshall felt exercising domination over them.

The same grim scene would replay itself regularly until that fateful sweltering summer night in 1970. On the sultry afternoon of August 3, 1970, Gwendolyn had let Allen, Ricky and Larry go to the swimming pool in Hogansville with a neighbor. Allen knew when his father had shown up at the pool and ordered him and his brothers out of the water and into the car that Marshall had come home early and discovered his mother's treat for the boys. Allen had no doubt that this had brought quick retribution to his mother at his father's hand.

Upon arriving back home, Allen quickly realized that something was different. He fully expected to find his mother in the house recovering from the results of his father's rage. The house, however, was empty except for the baby, Dean, who was lying in the crib. This fact seemed to shake his father as well, but for different reasons. Marshall could ill afford to have Gwendolyn begging for help throughout the neighborhood with her eyes swollen shut. He immediately told Allen to find her and come get him when he did.

Allen would find his mother and, in doing so, would take on the burden of guilt that would plague him for the rest of his life. It festered and ate at his soul much like an innocent man's horror at being sentenced to a life in prison for a crime he did not commit.

The image was forever burned into his mind. Just as he had thought, his mother had sought refuge at the Turners' house, and Allen located her in the hiding place she used many times in the past. The stale odor of the crawlspace met him as he opened the scuttle door and climbed under the house and into complete darkness. He switched on the flashlight that Mike Thrower had given him. The crawlspace diminished in height as he made his way from the rear of the house toward the front. With the beam piercing the darkness, he crept farther into this forbidding hell.

Approaching the center of the house, Allen could make out his mother's soft sobs. The light found her propped against a discarded space heater that had been tossed under the house in years past. Although Allen expected his mother to bear the signs of her torment, he was nauseated by what he found. Her left eye was swollen completely shut, and her right was a mere slit through which she peered as she heard the approach of her eldest son.

"Don't worry, Mama. I won't tell him," Allen's words struggled to the surface as he choked back his own tears.

"I'll get help and come back for you and your brothers. Just go back home and take care of them 'til I come back. Son, I love you." Those were the last words Allen would ever hear his mother say. As he slipped from under the house, Allen could hear his father cursing and calling out for Gwendolyn as he again stalked his prey.

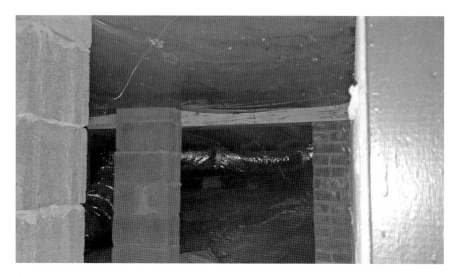

Crawlspace under the Turner House where Gwendolyn was hiding the night of her death. *Author's collection.*

The next time Allen would see his mother would be when he stared down at her lifeless body at the bottom of her garbage-strewn tomb. It would be these awful images that would haunt him for the rest of his life.

Allen was certain that, any day, there would be a knock at the door and the sheriff or the GBI agent he had spoken with would be there to arrest his father. As awful as that would be, it would be only right. There was no way that what happened to his mother could be ignored. The sad truth was that in 1970 Troup County, it was not just ignored—it was consciously disregarded.

Just over three months after Gwendolyn was found in the well, Marshall remarried a young, attractive divorcée named Priscilla Shepherd. Priscilla's father was Robert Shepherd, a man known to have his hands in many questionable enterprises in Troup County. He was also said to have Sheriff Lem Bailey in his pocket.

One afternoon six months after Gwendolyn's death, Allen was in the yard with his father as Marshall worked on the family car. Allen never knew what he had done exactly, but something set Marshall off. He went into a rage and started pummeling Allen in the face with his fists. Allen crumpled to the ground. Marshall took off his shoe and beat Allen over the head with it. At some point, Allen broke free and bolted toward the Turners' house, diving over the short fence between the yards.

Ronnie Turner and Mike Thrower, both fifteen-year-old friends of Allen's, were in the Turners' yard. It was nothing new for them to see Allen run to safety; they had watched for nearly three years as Marshall had beaten Gwendolyn and the children. To both boys, who had always been treated kindly by Allen's mother and had seen firsthand the brutality of Marshall Moore, this was the last straw. Cursing Allen from the fence, Marshall ordered his son back into his yard, threatening to beat the hell out of him if he didn't return immediately. With those threats wafting through the air, Mike went inside the house, got his father's shotgun and propped it against the porch. Ronnie stepped in front of Allen. "If you step one foot into our yard, I'm going to shoot you," he told Marshall Moore, a man who not only personified "mean" but also practically tripled him in size. The young man's steady threat and the gun leaning against the porch kept Marshall at bay. Beaten and bloody, Allen was lying on the Turners' floor when the sheriff's deputies arrived.

When told of Marshall's assault on Allen, the officers offered Allen the same protection they had offered his mother: he could go home to his father's wrath or he could leave. Allen knew there was nothing he could do to protect his brothers. He opted for the only chance he felt he had. He left, walking.

It was fifteen miles to LaGrange. Allen knew that if he could get to his aunt's house on Hill Street, he would find refuge there. He was sore and stiff from the beating Marshall had issued him, but he made the distance in three hours.

Aunt Siene was the wife of Marshall's brother, Joe. She had witnessed and experienced firsthand the brutality of the Moore clan. She and Joe were divorced, but she had known and loved Gwendolyn's children and was willing to do what she could to protect Allen from his tormentor.

Siene opened her home to Allen and told him he could stay as long as he either attended school or got a job to support himself. Allen felt the need to become independent as soon as possible. His father had never placed a premium on schoolwork, so his scholarship was somewhat lacking. And there was the major stumbling block on his road to employment: who would hire a fourteen-year-old boy?

Allen knew that he would have to be resourceful if he was going to make it on his own. He obtained a copy of his birth certificate and, with a few minor alterations, became old enough to qualify for employment at the Dixie Cotton Mill in LaGrange. Allen worked in the mill for three years, earning a reputation as a hard worker and a good young man.

It wasn't long, however, before he began to yearn for something more in his life. The memory of his mother and his life as a child tortured him. He felt a need to escape the life he was making for himself in the cotton mill. Although he was making a fair wage for someone lacking a high school diploma, he wanted to put distance between himself and his past in hopes of attaining much-needed relief from those haunting memories. He found that opportunity with the U.S. Navy.

With Aunt Siene's blessing, Allen joined the U.S. Navy in 1973. He quickly earned his high school equivalency certificate and was on course for a long and successful military career. He persevered. He became a good sailor, and his professional career was going extremely well. But old ghosts from the past would not leave him alone. He still woke up in a cold sweat in the middle of most nights, jolted awake by nightmares of his childhood. The nightmares found him still trying to bear the responsibility for his mother's death.

The adult Allen Moore did not fare well in his relationships with women. He was never physically abusive, but the lack of a decent model for successful husband/wife relationships led to four marriages and just as many divorces. Allen often wondered if he truly knew how to love someone deeply. The only person he had ever loved was his mother. He knew that he would never recover from her loss, so he made the conscious decision never to expose himself to that kind of pain again. In his relationships, he never gave of himself completely.

Allen's naval career came to a successful conclusion in 1993. He retired as a full chief petty officer, the highest rank of enlisted men. Maybe it was the distance from his past, or maybe it was his dogged determination to be

different, but whatever the case may be, Allen had throttled forward from A to Z. Although tortured by the relentless demons from his past, he had become a decent and kind man. From time to time, he would succumb to those demons, and his only avenue of escape would be to drown them. But even with the drinking, Allen managed to hold it in check.

While in the navy, Allen developed an affinity for electronics. When it came to maintaining sophisticated electronic systems, he had become a bit of a wizard. After his discharge, he found what he thought to be a good fit in civilian life.

Allen Moore. *Allen Moore.*

He took a job at Cornell Corrections Facility, a large prison in Folkston, Georgia. His high military security clearances and work ethic ensured that he was a person who earned trust in a secure environment. Allen again rose to the top of his field and was soon the superintendent over all electronic surveillance for facilities in the region.

Over the years, Al, as he was now known, was able to keep his demons at arm's length, but they were always hovering just below the surface. He was never able to find the closure he so desperately needed. He had come to grips with the fact that the truth would never be told. Those who knew the truth were either too ashamed to discuss it or not in a position to do anything about it.

So, on a beautiful autumn morning in October 2002, as he leaned back in the comfort of his chair in the peaceful seclusion of his office, Allen had no idea when the phone rang that the voice on the other end would catapult him back to the scorching heat of that August morning thirty-two years earlier, when he stood devastated beside that garbage-strewn pit, his mother's first grave. A child once again hearing his mother's anguished cries from the well.

DERAILING THE
GOOD OL' BOY MACHINE

Watching twenty years of Sheriff Bailey's brand of justice was about all Buddy could stand. The law was being used to run roughshod over the very ones who needed its protection the most, people like Gwendolyn Moore. Gwendolyn's murder was the most blatant case of the law being ignored to suit the whims of political cronies that Buddy had ever seen. Other than neighbors who were outraged by the obvious lack of security afforded to her during her life, no one seemed to be interested in seeking justice for Gwendolyn. The more Buddy thought of her tortured death, the more he became filled with a resolve to do whatever was necessary to put law back into the hands of the citizens of Troup County.

"Trooper, I think I'm going to run for the sheriff's office next year," Daddy said as we rode out Highway 54 through the small community of Harrisonville. I was a state trooper working out of the LaGrange Post of the Georgia State Patrol. Every night, I worked in Troup County, and when his schedule allowed, Buddy rode with me. He was friends with Major Hugh Hardison, the commanding officer of the Georgia State Patrol, and had permission to ride with any trooper on patrol, as long as the trooper welcomed him. In my case, he was always welcome; some of our greatest camaraderie came as we rode together and talked.

While we drove, our conversations covered every topic, but many revolved around the injustices of our local arena and the havoc they wreaked on the citizens of our county. Buddy had talked of running for sheriff in 1976, but at that time, his personal demon of alcohol addiction was still a day-to-day battle to overcome. Also, he did not have the financial backing at the time to run a credible race. Knowing this, Sheriff Bailey came to see Buddy when the election rumor mill began to churn and Buddy's name was mentioned as a contender.

"Now Buddy, I plan to hold office for one more term and then retire," Sheriff Bailey said. "Your chances of getting elected, should you decide to run, will be much better with me out of the race. I know many of my people up in your area that will wholeheartedly support you with me out of the picture."

Buddy was fully aware of how the machine worked, and he knew that beating it would be a formidable task. But he wasn't sure, with his alcoholism being fresh in people's minds, if the time was right. He deferred running for office, not because of the sheriff's visit but because he wanted to be 100 percent sure that all aspects of his life were in order for such a huge undertaking. The election of 1980 would be the right time; however, to no one's surprise, the Boys convinced Sheriff Bailey to reverse his commitment not to seek reelection. They weren't about to let their cash cow out of the barn.

"You know it's going to be tough with Sheriff Bailey deciding to run for another term," I warned as we rode west. "That unlimited supply of money from the Boys and help from the Democratic Committee will make it an uphill battle."

"I've decided it's now or never, son. I know the time is right. People have taken the brunt of their Boss Hogg politics for too long. It's got this county by the throat," Buddy said.

"Chief, you know there's a millstone around your neck that you're going to have to deal with," I said, referring to his past drinking. "It's the only thing the Boys have to come at you with."

Lem Bailey campaign card, 1980. *Del Kulhman Private Collection.*

"Well, it's the truth, and I can't ignore it or run from it. I'll just face it and assert it myself and take it away from them," Buddy declared with dogged determination.

In the spring of 1980, when he announced his candidacy, Buddy Bryant did so as a recovering alcoholic in a newspaper announcement. His platform was simple: the office of the sheriff would be fair and responsive to everyone in Troup County. The office would not be run by the Machine in the Boss Hogg fashion of the past.

I did not realize how many people had awakened to the politics of the Machine and its ways of lining the pockets of the few. Support for Buddy grew rapidly. And even though it was a five-man race, it was evident that he was the man to beat. He had a good organization headed by Tommie Norred, a young man who worked for Southern Bell. Together, they worked tirelessly toward their goal.

The Machine had been in power far too long. Its corruption and influence were even greater than I had known at the time or would come to know in the future. What made the Machine vulnerable was the belief that the system was undefeatable. This fact would prove to be its undoing.

Spring drifted into summer, the hottest summer on record in our part of Georgia. Nearly every day of June, July and August 1980, the mercury climbed to the century mark and above. With the help of his good friends and supporters, Buddy walked to almost every house in Troup County in that unrelenting heat over a three-month period to ask each citizen for his or her vote and support.

ON AUGUST 3, 1980, Buddy won his way into a runoff with the all-powerful Machine and was poised to take office by what some considered to a potential landslide. On the morning of August 18, 1980, as I was on my way to work, I stopped by to see him. He was in high spirits because every other candidate, with the exception of Sheriff Bailey, had endorsed him publicly since the primary. He was on course to achieve his dream. He told me he had to pay for some advertising in LaGrange and that afterward he would come home to rest and take a break from the heat.

"I feel tired, son, but I only have ten more days left," he said. "Then I can take some time off to recharge." I told him I'd stop by later that night and share a cup of coffee with him. I didn't drink coffee, but I always loved spending time and talking with him when he did. "Be careful, Trooper," he chided as I went out the door. "And don't drive that damn car so fast."

Buddy fell dead of a massive heart attack at 2:30 p.m. that afternoon. The years of smoking and drinking, coupled with the constant work and stress of his campaign that hot summer, had taken their toll. Mama was with him; she said he simply took one big breath, closed his eyes and that was that. She called the ambulance and they rushed him to the hospital, but he was gone. It was the third heart attack he had suffered and the last. I was devastated.

All the hard work Buddy had done had not been in vain. Much to the consternation of the Boys, who had immediately assumed that they had won by default, the law required that the third candidate be elevated back into the race. In an effort to finish the job of dislodging the Boys' grip on the county, Buddy's campaign committee met after his funeral and decided to support Gene Jones, a retired state patrol sergeant.

Gene was a good lawman, someone who would take the office in the right direction. The Sheriff's Office would no longer be used as a tool by a select few. On August 28, 1980, with the help of Buddy's supporters, Jones was elected by a comfortable margin. This was the beginning of the end of an old political dynasty. Sheriff Bailey had held the office for thirty-two years. Over the next few years, the remaining power left of the Boys in charge of the Democratic Executive Committee was scuttled by the new blood. The Boss Hogg era had come to an end.

Even with the very course of history changing in Troup County, it seemed as though the haunting memory of Gwendolyn Moore had died with Buddy. No one knew all that he had known about the case. And they did not know how to listen for the voice from the well.

My Road

Providence is a powerful force in our lives. There are certain circumstances that are just meant to be. It is my belief that some of us have destinies that are, in a sense, predetermined from birth. And if we have the dedication to follow the directions of our life's choosing, we can lead satisfying and successful lives.

I know now that I was born and raised to be a peace officer, but there was a time in my life when I made the decision to forge off into another direction. I resigned and tried for nearly ten years to distance myself from the profession. I was successful in other endeavors and made a good living. The problem? While the paycheck was sufficient, I was miserable.

I remain thoroughly convinced that my reentry into law enforcement was part of the will of the greater power that works in all our lives. Thank God for providence.

From the time I was old enough to remember, I was raised on the front seat of a police car and in the police station—not only by my parents but also with the help of about twenty law enforcement officers. Under the watchful eye of my father, I learned from them all. "Son," my daddy would say, "policemen are just like everybody in all walks of life. Take a pool of ten people—it doesn't matter if they are doctors, lawyers, millworkers or carpenters. Out of the ten, there will be one or two that will be outstanding, there will be six who are adequate and one or two will be totally worthless. You can learn from them all, even if it's how not to do something."

Trooper Clay Bryant, 1976. *Author's collection.*

As usual, Daddy was right. Dick Staley, Norman Smith, Marshall Cardwell, T. Horton, Charlie Frank Green, James Glenn and so many more of the policemen who worked the streets of Hogansville played essential parts in my raising.

Throughout my years in school, I always performed well academically and with minimal effort, probably to my detriment. Buddy, although he loved his profession, harbored the desire that I become a prosecutor. I had a problem with this because it was necessary to become a lawyer in order to become a prosecutor, and that was a vocation for which I had acquired a certain amount of disdain, although I now realize that derision was unwarranted.

All I wanted was to become a peace officer. This desire was fueled by a rather large case of hero worship for my dad, a weighty case that I continue to carry to this day. My father, on the other hand, wanted me to pursue a profession that would afford me greater wealth and a better quality of life than he felt law enforcement could offer. And so my dad held on to and vocalized his belief that my becoming a prosecutor would be the answer to both of these desires. I don't know what he was thinking, as I haven't seen any wealthy prosecutors in all my travels around prosecution offices in the state.

My father and Crawford Ware, our local representative in the state legislature, were extremely good friends. At the time, Mr. Ware had more seniority than any other member of the House, with the exception of House Speaker Tom Murphy. Mr. Ware was on many powerful committees and chaired the Appropriations Committee, which controlled the purse strings of state government. He used his influence well for his constituents, and he was happy to help my father advance the career of his son.

I applied for a job as a radio operator with the Georgia State Patrol before I graduated from high school. "Son, I'll help you get that job, but you've got to promise me you'll go on to school and get a degree," Buddy bargained. I agreed to go to college and graduated from Hogansville High School on May 31, 1973. I reported to the Georgia State Patrol Post in LaGrange the next day to begin my career.

I spent the next three years working the radio in LaGrange and attending college at the Georgia Police Academy three nights a week. In 1976, as soon as I turned twenty-one, I was promoted to trooper. That same year, Buddy hit me up to go to law school on his nickel. I was having the time of my life as a trooper, but I wasn't about to disappoint my father or my mother by not accepting their generous offer. I enrolled at the Woodrow Wilson School of Law in Atlanta and embarked on a daily pilgrimage to the school over the next three years.

In June 1980, I received a degree in law. It was the proudest day of my dad's life. My graduation day was the only day that I remember my dad taking a break from campaigning for sheriff that miserably hot summer. With several weighty endorsements from citizens as eager to usher local law enforcement into the twentieth century as he was, Buddy was becoming increasingly successful in his bid for the office of sheriff. Add the fact that his baby boy had graduated from law school and it was easy to see how these were truly the best of times for my father. Life was good. Then the unthinkable happened. In the middle of an election he was bound to win, my daddy died of a heart attack.

I was lost. He was my father and my best friend in the world. Everything I'd ever wanted for him looked like it was going in the right direction...and then *boom*. When Daddy died, a part of me and a great deal of direction for my life died as well. I stumbled around aimlessly for a few months, trying to lose myself in my job, but it just wasn't the same. In June 1981, the Hogansville City Council offered me my father's job, and for all the wrong reasons, I accepted it. I thought I would just take his place and it would be as though he never left.

I dearly loved Hogansville; it was my home. For the most part, the next ten years as chief of police were an enjoyable time. I was able to maintain a small but progressive police department. We ran the city's ambulance service out of the police department and made it an advanced life support service that served the northern end of Troup County. We built our own firing range and became the off-campus training location for the Regional Police Academy. We also operated our own drug stings and prosecuted all our own felony cases. We accomplished all this and more.

But there was still one overriding problem: I wasn't Buddy Bryant—I was Buddy's boy. My strength had become my weakness. The one thing of which I was most proud made me a prisoner to the legacy of my father. What a paradox. As time moved on, I realized that no matter what I accomplished, I would always be in Buddy's shadow. Folks in Hogansville wanted what they'd had, just like I wanted what I'd had. But the fact was that neither of us was going to have that again. Buddy was gone.

It's hard to understand how a person with all the support that had been afforded me could be at such a loss of direction. If only my daddy could have been with me to impart some of his age-old wisdom.

After a while, I had several good offers from larger departments looking for a young, well-educated and innovative police chief. Peachtree City, Fort Valley and others came calling, but I just couldn't bring myself to leave my hometown.

Hogansville, like many small textile towns in the South, became less and less progressive and began to struggle financially. The town mayor and city council began a turnover each election, producing an intractable, "Either yer fer me or agin me" political stance. This degenerated into a cutthroat mess that affected the entire city government; the police department was no exception.

My confrontational style didn't sit too well with the newly elected mayor who took office in 1992, Calvin Turbyfield. Calvin and I attended First Baptist Church together. When he ran for office, it was against a man who was openly gay. Calvin came to my office and told me, "Clay, I need you to help me get elected over that queer." I told Calvin I thought he'd be elected but that in my ten years there I had tried to distance myself from an active role in politics because no matter who won, I was still their police chief. Calvin failed to see the logic in this and said, "You might come to regret your decision."

Calvin was only half right. I never regretted my decision, but life with him as mayor was a bit strained for me as police chief. Buddy's wisdom was, "Son, never argue with a fool. People on the sideline won't be able to tell which one is which." When the city council agreed to give me one month's severance pay, I turned in my resignation in June 1992 and moved to LaGrange, where I began work as a paramedic supervisor with Troup County Emergency Medical Services.

I enjoyed the EMS, but it wasn't law enforcement. After three years of twenty-four-hour shifts, I realized that a long career with these hours was going to destroy my family life, a sacrifice I wasn't willing to make. I had missed policing every day since I resigned, but I refused to pursue my first love for fear of a political backlash.

I started my own tire business, and it began to do very well. I was selling for Bridgestone/Firestone, a company that saw the potential and eventually bought out my little business. Soon I went to work for Bridgestone/Firestone, but every time I was around my old policing friends, my heart would break.

In the fall of 2002, Roy Olinger, a retired GBI agent who had worked with the District Attorney's Office as a criminal investigator, mentioned to me that his old job there was open. He suggested I check into it. Hesitant at first, I figured they might not want an old peace officer who'd been out of the business for ten years.

I had known Pete Skandalakis, district attorney for the Coweta Judicial Circuit, for many years. Our law enforcement and prosecution careers had run parallel in years past while he was a DA and I was a young police officer. I had an honest respect for him as a man and as a prosecutor. I called Pete and asked if he would consider me for the position. He told me to apply.

The District Attorney's Office had evolved into the largest law firm in the Circuit, and an administrative manager was in charge of hiring employees. Apprehensive at first, I took the plunge and applied. I knew that I wanted to finish my life's work where it had begun: in law enforcement. In mid-October 2003, I was hired and soon doing again what I loved most. Little did I know how much my life was about to change, influenced by the powers of the past.

As I sat at my desk only nine days after being hired by the DA's Office, the phone rang. It was Larry Arrington, an investigator for the Sheriff's Office. Larry, a friend of mine, knew I had a fair amount of knowledge of local history and asked if I remembered a case in the Hogansville area from years before where a woman's body had been recovered from an abandoned well on Mobley Bridge Road. I told Larry that not only was I familiar with it but also that I was there when she was recovered from the well. He related to me that there was no record of it at the Sheriff's Office; he went on to say that a young lady named Leslie Power had found a death certificate of a relative she did not even know existed, and it was marked as a homicide. Ms. Power had inquired as to the findings in the case, and Larry, unable to find any record of the event, faxed me a copy of the death certificate along with Leslie Power's phone number in the hope that I would be able to give her any details I might have known.

As I read the death certificate in my hand, my mind replayed the scenes from long ago. I could see Daddy saying, "If only they had lived across the road." My gaze fell on the top of the faxed sheets I had just received. They were dated October 24, 2002. The significance was not lost on me—it was my father's birthday. In the twenty-two years since his death, there had not been a time that I had failed to remember his birthday. I guess with the new job and my mind being so preoccupied with it, Daddy's birthday had slipped my mind. I can only assume that this was his way of bringing it to my attention.

I sat dumbfounded in my chair as thoughts raced through my mind. Suddenly it all came flooding back—the sights and sounds of a wretched summer day in 1970—and I felt as if I could hear my father's voice telling me to listen for that small, long-silenced voice that was crying out from the well.

Gwendolyn's Path to the Well

Gwendolyn Moore was born on April 28, 1940, to Flora and Rassie Lee McDaniel, the fourth of five living children; her brother Campwell had died from a liver ailment the year before, just months after his birth in 1939.

Flora and Rassie were old school, brought up on the age-old southern principles of hard work, independence and the sanctity of family. They raised their children to respect these same values, unaware that by doing so those revered beliefs would subject their baby girl to a life of total domination, maniacal control, horrific violence and, in the end, her death.

Rassie Lee was a quiet, hardworking man—by all accounts a dependable, decent, God-fearing man and a good father. He worked for the Southern Railroad at the Atlanta Rail Yard, known today as Inman Yard, in southeast Atlanta. Not one to carouse and party, Rassie Lee kept to himself when he wasn't at work. His life away from the rail yard was spent quietly with Flora and the children.

Pat Terry, Rassie's middle daughter, would describe their life to others as "wonderful. We worked hard and we were taught respect. Daddy was a gentle and kind person; I never knew him to raise a hand toward our mother. He worked every day, and on Friday or Saturday night, he might take a drink, but come Sunday morning, he had on his suit and was straight as an arrow. Even if [he] didn't go to church, he'd never drink on Sunday or during the week."

Times were hard in the 1940s and early 1950s for a working-class family in Adamsville, a small community just outside Atlanta's West End. Rassie Lee worked to provide a simple but comfortable life for Flora and their children.

Flora McDaniel was a no-nonsense, hardworking woman. Like Rassie Lee, Flora grew up in what would be considered a "poor" family. But where they were short on money and possessions, they were rich in character and decency. Flora was raised with an extra measure of southern self-reliance. She lived her life for her husband and children while operating under the belief that everyone else did the same. She didn't work outside the home, but she certainly worked. She maintained three large gardens every summer, canned all the family's food

Gwendolyn Moore's school picture from Margaret Fain Middle School, circa 1950. *Pat Terry Private Collection.*

and tended the chickens, hogs and the family milk cow. She also took in sewing from the community to help out—all while raising five children. She was straightforward and raised her children to be the same, demanding that they be dedicated to the family and that each contribute his or her fair share.

During this era, decent families raised their children to become self-sufficient, encouraging them to find a good mate, work hard, dedicate themselves to the family and raise their own children in the same traditions. Children were taught to work out problems on their own. As wonderful a foundation as it was, this philosophy for life had one major flaw: it relied on every other person in the world being as truthful and sincere as the McDaniels.

It was this imperfection, this candidness and otherwise exemplary way of life, that spelled disaster for Gwendolyn. The principles that dictated her life, and would have made her a wonderful life partner, also made her a perfect target for a man like Marshall Moore.

Just down the road from where Gwendolyn resided on Bankhead Highway, her friend Buck Jones lived with his parents. The Joneses ran a small café on the west side of Atlanta. One year, they took in a young, troubled runaway from the North Georgia Mountains named Marshall Moore. Moore lived with the Jones family for about four years, working for his room and board in the café and becoming acquainted with the folks of Adamsville.

Life in Adamsville was simple and uncomplicated. Gwendolyn was a kind and gentle soul, but she also had an impetuous side. Although devoted to her

Moore family photo, 1960. *Front, from left to right*: Larry, Ricky and Allen. *Rear*: Gwendolyn and Marshall. *Pat Terry Private Collection.*

family and their way of life, she was lively and longed for adventure. In the 1950s, working-class people in the South married off their children with the expectation that they start a family, so it was no surprise that Gwendolyn's thoughts turned toward finding a mate as a natural progression but also as a way to get out from under the strict eye of her mother. Gwendolyn's peaceful life in Adamsville took a dramatic and ultimately tragic turn when Marshall Moore set his cap for the pretty young daughter of Flora and Rassie Lee McDaniel. Was it in part Gwendolyn's delicate, petite frame that triggered the strong attraction Marshall felt for her? Doll-like in stature, with a heart-shaped pixie face, she would be no match physically for a man who dominated through the use of his size and strength.

To Gwendolyn, the handsome young stranger from the mountains held a certain amount of mystery along with his outward charm. Marshall was brash and captivating, nothing like the reserved young boys from the West End. After a brief courtship, the handsome young mountaineer won Gwendolyn's heart. She was so enamored of Marshall that she committed to marrying him long before she had gotten to know him. Standing next to Marshall, the top of Gwendolyn's head barely passed his shoulder. Perhaps she perceived his muscular, towering build as a symbol of the protection and strength he would provide as a mate. Little did she know that the one she believed would be a source of safety and security would, in fact, bestow on her constant fear as the creator of her own private Hell. Flora and Rassie Lee raised no objections to the marriage; they, too, failed to recognize how menacing the future would become for their beloved daughter. The McDaniels took folks as they appeared, and Marshall Moore seemed to be a hardworking, decent young man. Flora was therefore quite surprised when Mrs. Jones confided that Marshall had some deep-rooted problems and needed help before something awful happened. Unfortunately for all involved, Mrs. Jones did not elaborate, and Flora did not ask for further explanation.

On September 9, 1955, Gwendolyn and Marshall were married in a church ceremony in Adamsville. What shortly followed that day of celebration was Marshall's dark side, having been held in check long enough for him to gain his prize, surging forth and breaking through the façade. Gwendolyn's middle sister, Pat, was the first to see the results of his sinister traits. What she saw were the just the beginning pieces of evidence of what would become a regular occurrence in Gwendolyn's life. In a 2002 interview, Pat recalled the first time she saw her sister after her marriage to Marshall: "Gwendolyn had always been such a pretty girl, but when I went in to see her, her face was swollen and her front teeth were gone. I asked, 'What in the world happened to your face?' Gwendolyn weakly replied, 'Marshall beat me and knocked my teeth out.' Gwen and I were very close, but I couldn't stand to go around and see what he was doing to her. It seemed like almost every time I visited, she would be bruised all up or her eyes would be black and swollen."

Gwendolyn's former life had been anchored in the love of family life and stability that Rassie Lee and Flora provided. Her new life with Marshall Moore could only be described as nomadic and terror-filled, marked mostly by childbirths and beatings. When first married, they moved into a small apartment Marshall had in Adamsville, but they lived there only a very short period of time. In late 1955, the couple moved to a house on Purgason Mill Road out from Atlanta's West End. The couple was living there when their first son, Allen, was born on August 12, 1956. Marshall was beginning to ply his trade as a truck driver then, but times were hard for the young couple financially and they could not make ends meet. According to her family members, Gwendolyn was usually the target of Marshall's frustration. At the time, Rassie Lee had no idea what was happening to his little girl. Gwendolyn had been raised with Flora's philosophy that a husband and wife's business should be private and worked out at home. Rassie Lee could see the difficulty they were having, and after Allen was born, he offered them the basement apartment of the McDaniel house.

Gwendolyn was happy to be back near the comfort of her childhood, but Marshall was not as elated. He resented Gwendolyn and Allen being in full view of her family, enabling them to monitor his treatment of his wife and child. To Marshall, it was all about control, and with this turn of events, he felt that his dominance of every aspect of their lives was in jeopardy. Gwendolyn was forbidden to have regular contact with her parents, even though they were under the same roof. Rassie Lee could not understand why Gwendolyn had become so detached from their lives. Little did he know that his youngest child paid a heavy price for the contact she quietly tried to maintain with her parents. Any situation that Marshall disliked was dealt with swiftly and brutally, and interaction with her family topped the list of his dislikes.

In October, a family tragedy of epic proportions sealed Gwendolyn's fate. If ever there were to be an intervention by anyone in the McDaniel clan, it would come from Rassie Lee, for he was the more emotional and openly affectionate of the parents. At the time, though, Gwendolyn had done a superior job of keeping her father in the dark about the savagery she suffered at Marshall's hand. On October 3, 1956, Rassie Lee lost control of his car and hit a bridge abutment on Cascade Road in west Atlanta, leaving him paralyzed from the neck down. He was hospitalized for a few weeks until he was stable enough to return home. His prognosis was grave: he would be paralyzed for life, and his other injuries would bring complications that would result in his death. Gwendolyn was not allowed to go upstairs to comfort her father on his deathbed unless she slipped to his bedside unbeknownst to Marshall.

On March 8, 1957, while undergoing surgery to remove his legs, Rassie Lee died—along with Gwendolyn's chance for the support and strength she would need to escape her fate. After Rassie Lee passed away, Flora had to revert to her hard work ethic and resourcefulness. She sold her home in Adamsville and bought a small café and store in South Fulton County near Fairburn to support herself and her youngest son, David. Rassie Lee had made decent money while working for the Southern Railroad, but now the role of sole supporter fell on Flora's shoulders.

With the sale of her mother's house in Adamsville, Gwendolyn and Marshall were forced to find other accommodations; their transition needed to be done quickly because Gwendolyn was pregnant with her second child. The family moved into a small house on Gordon Road in west Atlanta. This was their home when Ricky was born on September 18, 1957. By this time, Gwendolyn's situation with Marshall had grown much worse, and she felt that she could not turn to her mother, who was dealing with major issues of her own. Gwendolyn was effectively isolated from the support of her family.

Gwendolyn's mother-in-law, Maude, had gotten to know Gwendolyn during the few occasions when Marshall took his wife and children to North Georgia to visit the family he had abandoned. Maude Moore was a kind and gentle woman, herself a victim of the violent tradition of wife beating and family abuse that followed the Moore men.

As a boy, Marshall had acquired a reputation for being a ruffian and bully who preyed on the weaknesses of others, even within his own family. Maude recognized Gwendolyn as the kind and tender girl she had been and knew that her daughter-in-law was suffering at Marshall's hand. She took Gwendolyn aside during one of the infrequent visits and told her that if she ever needed a place to escape to, she was welcome at Maude's home.

Gwendolyn also became close to Marshall's baby sister, Rose. "She was the kindest, sweetest person, totally devoted to her children, a wonderful mother," Rose said in taped interviews conducted in 2002. "It would break my heart to see her after Marshall had beaten her. She never deserved that."

After the death of her father, Gwendolyn did find herself seeking refuge with Maude. On more than one occasion, Marshall's family took in Gwendolyn and the boys. They came to know and love Gwendolyn and appreciate her as the devoted mother of their grandsons.

One time, Gwendolyn appeared at Maude's home with her eyes nearly swollen shut. Marshall's sister, Rose, and his first cousin Ruth Watts were sitting on the porch when Marshall arrived to retrieve her as if she were a runaway dog. Ruth recalled, "Marshall drove up with another woman in the car and got out taking his belt off as he walked toward the house and shouted as he approached, 'I'm gonna whip your ass until you get your ass and them damn young'uns in this car, and we're going back to Atlanta.' I had hated him since we were kids, when he used to beat and bully us. I told him, unless he was going to whip all of us, the thing for him to do was to get back in that car with his girlfriend and go on back to Atlanta. He knew I meant what I said; he got in that car and left cussing at us all. But he came back later the next week when everyone was at work and took Gwendolyn and the kids back home."

In 1959, Marshall moved Gwendolyn and the boys into Blair Village, a large government housing project on Atlanta's west side. They were living there when Larry was born on December 29, 1959. "Every time we would go by to check on Gwendolyn and the kids, Marshall would be gone in the truck, and Gwendolyn would be there alone with the children," her sister, Pat, recalled. "She would always be bruised and beat up. Sometimes, handfuls of hair would be gone."

Allen, with the pain of his childhood still evident in his voice, related how brutal his father was:

> Daddy could always find a reason to beat Mama. If supper were cold, Mama got beat. If supper was wrong, Mama got beat. If Daddy overslept, Mama got beat. If Mama woke him up too early, she got beat. Once I saw Mama get beat for not ironing fast enough to suit him. The thing that haunts me to this day was the fact that when Daddy would work himself into a rage, even if it was with one of us kids, Mama would step in and let him take it out on her instead of us, just to keep him from beating us. Daddy never just slapped her or hit her once. He beat her to the ground or until she was out cold. He enjoyed it, and he had kind of a ritual about it. He'd tear her clothes off, I guess so he could see the damage he was doing. Maybe it was just to degrade her. Then he would hit her with his fist. When she would go down, he'd pick her up by the hair to hit her again.

Mama wouldn't try to fight back. Sometimes she would beg him to not hit her anymore, but it seemed like that made him even worse.

In late 1961, Flora sold her café in Fairburn and moved to Mableton, another town just outside Atlanta's city limits. After one particularly violent episode, Gwendolyn went against her ingrained upbringing and called her mother for help. To Gwendolyn's surprise, Flora gladly opened her house to her daughter, as it was now clear to her just how desperate the situation had become. After she and the boys had been at Flora's for a few weeks, and after a series of threats and intimidation from Marshall, Flora came home from work one afternoon to find her back door kicked in and her pistol on the kitchen counter. Gwendolyn and the boys were gone. Frantic, yet knowing that there was nothing she could do, Flora waited to hear from her daughter. Later that day, Marshall called and wanted to bring Gwendolyn over to talk things out. When they arrived, Gwendolyn, as if reciting her lines from a script, told her mother that she had to go back home, and Flora relented.

In mid-1962, Flora and Pat received a call to come to the Old Austell Hospital, a private medical facility operated by Dr. Jack Bussey in Austell, a community bordering Powder Springs, where Marshall and Gwendolyn then lived. Upon arriving at the hospital, Flora was told that Gwendolyn had lost her baby, a seven-month-old fetus. "When I got there, Mama called me off to the side and said Gwendolyn had told her Marshall had kicked her in the stomach and left, and that the baby was dead," Pat recalled. "Gwen was in a terrible way. She cried and screamed all night while she delivered that poor dead baby."

Marshall never showed his face at the hospital. Roy Davis of the Roy Davis Funeral Home in Austell prepared the baby in a handmade coffin that he built himself. Gwendolyn's brother, David, and Pat's husband, Grady Terry, dug the child's grave at the Sweetwater Church in Paulding County in the family plot. David later commented, "He never even came to his baby's funeral."

After the funeral, Flora took Gwendolyn home to Powder Springs. Marshall was gone, but Siene, Marshall's sister-in-law, was there. She and her husband, Joe, had moved in with Marshall and Gwendolyn. Siene had befriended Gwendolyn and promised Flora and Pat that she would take care of Gwendolyn—she had also suffered the legacy of abuse by a Moore son. The boys had been taken to Marshall's mother's house until Gwendolyn recovered. Marshall contended that the baby wasn't his, and after Gwendolyn began to have her miscarriage, he left.

According to Allen, from the mid-'60s until her death, his mother was beaten two or three times a week on a regular basis. Furthermore, Allen said that Marshall's tendency for violence toward his sons increased as well. The doctor who treated Gwendolyn following these beatings told Flora that if Gwendolyn continued to be subjected to these beatings, permanent brain damage would be the result.

This time, Gwendolyn tried to listen to her mother and sister. She got her boys and sought refuge at her sister's home in Douglas County. In April 1966, Pat took Gwendolyn to a lawyer in Douglasville who drafted a petition for divorce. He instructed Gwendolyn to file the divorce papers in DeKalb County. After hearing Gwendolyn's account of her marriage, the lawyer told her, "If you don't go through with this, he will kill you." After visiting the lawyer, Gwendolyn and Pat returned to Douglasville. Pat planned to take Gwendolyn to the courthouse in Decatur to file her divorce later that week.

In front of Pat's home that week, utility construction was in progress. When the workmen were not present, the neighborhood children found it a wonderful place to play in the shallow ditch, with piles of dirt resembling makeshift mountains. On one particular day, Gwendolyn's boys Ricky and Larry, along with Pat's daughter, Sandra, were in the yard playing when, according to Sandra, "a car came flying into the yard."

Marshall got out, stood behind the door and hollered at the kids, "Y'all get your damn ass in this car." At about that time, Allen and Tony, Pat's son, came from behind the house. Sandra, Larry and Ricky started to cry, and Larry sobbed, "I want to stay with Mama." According to Sandra, Marshall yelled, "I said get in this goddamned car before I beat the hell out of all of you!" All three boys were squalling as they climbed into the car.

Gwendolyn, who had been inside when she heard the commotion, ran out the front door. Marshall stood behind the car door and bellowed, "I'll be back in ten minutes, and if you ain't got your shit ready to go, I'll kill these damn young'uns." Marshall tore out of the driveway and within minutes came flying by, blowing the horn. A few minutes later, he pulled back into the yard, where Gwendolyn had her and her sons' clothes lying in the driveway. Terrified that he would hurt her babies, she got in the car with the monster that was her husband.

Following those events, Marshall Moore moved Gwendolyn and the boys to Troup County and rented a house on Overbrook Drive, just off US 29, south of LaGrange. Debra Merna Grizzard, a young girl at the time but now an investigator for the Heard County Sheriff's Department, was a neighbor. She recalled, "He was so mean to her. We were just teenagers, but

Gwendolyn Moore in her casket, August 5, 1970. *Pat Terry Private Collection.*

at night, you could hear her crying and begging him not to hit her. We would ask the boys if Gwendolyn was all right, and they always said she was okay. But he treated her awful. If he wasn't beating her, it was constant cursing and yelling."

In 1968, Marshall and Gwendolyn moved once again. The house was just outside the city limits of Hogansville, in unincorporated Troup County, on Mobley Bridge Road at the intersection of Lee Street. It was here where baby Dean was born on July 17, 1969. This was also the house where Gwendolyn would live out the remainder of her tortured life. In later years, Allen would describe his mother's existence as "being a prisoner and a slave."

It's almost impossible to comprehend how a man, a human being, could ever be so evil to another, especially when that evil is exacted on the ones he should cherish the most: the man's wife and children.

THE LEGACY

What part of a man, a human being, can cause evil to take hold and win over decency and mercy? Is it a learned trait, or is it a flaw innate to some people's character that can never be reversed? In the case of Marshall Moore, it may have been both.

In the northeastern corner of Georgia lie the foothills of the Great Smoky Mountains, and it is in the midst of this breathtaking scenery that you will find Appalachia, a region long known in American folklore for its impoverished lifestyle. To this day, Appalachia is recognized as one of the most economically and socially deprived areas of the United States. The mountainous terrain is unforgiving and does not lend itself well to agriculture, which was historically the primary vocation of the poorer inhabitants of the region. The life of a sharecropper in the mountains of North Georgia was a hard life indeed, and those who endured it sometimes became hardened and desensitized to the people and world surrounding them.

Such was the birthright of the Moore family, dating back to before the Civil War. From the faces of the rocky hillsides of Banks and Rabun Counties, the Moore clan attempted to chisel out a living from the substandard terrain surrounding Bogg's Mountain. This was a corner of the state where local governments could ill afford to offer adequate law enforcement and education programs, let alone social assistance programs. What was known as the "Code of the Hills" prevailed, recognized throughout the region as the law of the land. Abiding by this system, a man ruled his family at his own discretion, and no one interfered with another family's sovereignty.

On a cool day in 1924, two siblings—young J.P. and his sister, Mary—were in the yard of the old house at the foot of Bogg's Mountain when they heard the sounds of a violent altercation riding the breeze from the house. It was the distinctive sound of hand hitting flesh, followed by the agonized cries of their mother, Sara Jane Teems Moore. Sara Jane was screaming and begging her husband, Joseph Alexander Moore, not to hit her again. Battered and bloody, Sara Jane bolted from the door and ran crying up the hill toward Bogg's Mountain. In a blind rage, the children's father yelled for them to go to their grandfather's house down the road. Then he bellowed that he was going to get their maw.

Terrified, the children ran to their grandfather's. They waited, but their parents did not come home that evening. From the porch of their grandfather's house on Bogg's Mountain, they could see the glow of a big fire on the side of the mountain. As the smoke and fog settled into the valley, the nauseating and unforgettable stench of burning flesh floated down with it. Joseph came back home and announced that Sara would not be returning.

Later, human remains were found in a fire pit on the mountain. No one ever questioned what had happened to Sara Jane—no one had need. To Joseph Moore and those like him who subscribed to the Code of the Hills, it was his inalienable right to exact his version of the law on his own family, as they were his property to do with as he wished.

After the death of their mother, J.P. and Mary were raised by their father in the same tradition as he had been raised. Mary became a child bride like most of the young girls of the region. J.P. took a child bride of his own, marrying Maude Smith in Rabun County in 1936. On March 18, 1937, Marshall, the first child of their six children, was born, followed by Joe, Ernest, Robert, Ray and Rose, the only girl.

Rose recalled:

Memories of our childhood were more like nightmares. One of the first memories that I can vividly recall was Daddy coming in the house. We were dirt poor, and I was just three or four years old, but I remember it like it was yesterday. I was on Mama's lap sitting by the wood stove when he came in. He had his boots tied with wire because he couldn't afford store-bought laces. As he pulled his overalls over the boots, the wire snagged his overalls and ripped a hole in the leg. Daddy went into a rage, threw the overalls into the fire, and spun around and slapped Mama, knocking her and me out the chair. He slapped her several times and made her sit in the chair while he cussed and beat her. He got the kerosene jug we used to start the fire with and threatened to set her on fire. He continued to beat and slap Mama until he got tired of it. Daddy gave the kerosene jug to Joe, who was about twelve or thirteen at the time, and told him, "If the bitch moves, burn her." Joe stood guard, not knowing what to do until Daddy finally calmed down.

"Similar ordeals were regular occasions throughout our childhood," Rose continued. "Mama finally got some relief in 1955 when Daddy got caught burglarizing a place in Banks County. During the burglary, he had poor Joe drive the car, and when Daddy went to the chain gang, Joe got sent to reform school at Alto because of Daddy."

When J.P. got out of prison, he went home to Maude. His sadistic behavior quickly resumed, with recurring instances of brutalizing Maude and terrorizing the children. After one particularly vicious attack, J.P. told Maude to get out. She took the children and fled, determined to make a life for herself and her two youngest children, Rose and Ray. She was able to keep J.P. away and filed for divorce, successfully breaking the cycle with her younger children.

Before Maude's unexpected death of natural causes in 1984, she had confided to Rose, "Whatever happens when I die, I already have a plot at home in Lakemont in the cemetery there. Don't let them bury me with your daddy. I have lived through one hell with him, and I sure don't want to spend eternity with him." After her death, Maude's wishes were carried out.

According to family members, Marshall, even as a young man, was an intimidating figure. "He was mean," recalled his cousin, Ruth. "Even as a kid, he would bully us around. He and his brothers were constantly fighting with each other and everyone else. When Marshall left home and went to Atlanta, it was a relief for us kids."

Marshall was determined that he didn't want any part of life in the North Georgia Mountains. He left home at the young age of fourteen, making his way to Atlanta, where he was sure the hustle and bustle of the city would be more to his liking than the rocky hills of Rabun County. It was in Adamsville, in Atlanta's West End, where he made a friend in young Buck Jones. Buck's family took him in—a decision they would later regret.

Marshall's behavior was not just about violence, but rather total control and domination. After he met and married Gwendolyn in 1955, he immediately set about fulfilling his need to be in complete control, assuming the role of the classic batterer. He would strike out in rage when he felt the least bit threatened, much like a caged animal—almost always, the object of his rage was Gwendolyn. In the early years after the beatings began,

Gwendolyn would seek shelter with Marshall's mother, as she was ashamed for her family to know of her plight.

Despite the increasing violence, Marshall could always seek her out, and using the charm that first caught her attention, he would convince her to take him back, reassuring her that he had changed and that he did the awful things he did out of his boundless love for her. Gwendolyn wanted to believe that, for she so badly wanted to raise her family in the traditions of her father. Marshall, in the traditions of *his* father, viewed Gwendolyn as property, his possession to be controlled and used in any way he desired. As their children came along, Marshall saw them in the same light. He used the boys as a tool of absolute control over Gwendolyn. He knew that the depth of her devotion to her sons knew no bounds, and it would be that unconditional love that would time and again hold her hostage to Marshall and her inescapable life of misery.

As the boys grew older, Marshall's propensity for violence toward them increased. The only way Gwendolyn could keep the boys out of harm's way was to intercede, acting as a decoy and physically placing herself between Marshall and the children whenever his rage surfaced.

As a textbook case batterer, Marshall had to feel total control over all aspects of his life. If for some reason he felt threatened or insecure about a situation, he would answer those feelings with the compelling need to execute total domination over those he felt were his possessions. As a result, Gwendolyn became the major outlet for the shortcomings in Marshall's world. This was a role in which no one could have remained and survived.

The lessons of generations of violence and abuse that were cast on this family of men by their fathers would prove to be the undoing of their families, each in its own time. The legacy of brutality inherent in Joseph would, in turn, be passed down to his sons and would ultimately wreak havoc on the lives of future generations. Some fifty years later, this legacy would also end the life of his grandson's wife, Gwendolyn.

However, something unforeseen, something unexpected, issued forth from the abandoned well in Hogansville. In death, Gwendolyn's voice rose from that well and was heard, begging for this horrible family legacy to no longer poison future generations.

Life and Death
on Mobley Bridge Road

Life on Mobley Bridge Road was a continuation of the same pattern of abuse for Gwendolyn. It was not long before the Moores' neighbors recognized the terrible results of Marshall's violent temper toward Gwendolyn and the children.

Ronnie Turner, a next-door neighbor, described Gwendolyn in a 2002 interview: "She was just a little bitty woman, and he was a big man…the meanest man I ever saw. The way he beat her and them boys, sometimes she would be so beat up she wouldn't come out to be seen for days at a time. We would ask Allen and Ricky how she was, and they would say she was too embarrassed to come outside with her face all messed up. Sometimes we would call the police when he would be beating her, but they couldn't do nothing because it was out of the city. When the sheriff's deputy came, they never did anything to him, and when they left, he would make her sorry they showed up."

Louise Turner and her husband, Junior, lived on the east side of the Moores' house. "She would show up on our porch all beat up and begging for help, and we'd hide her under our house to keep her from getting beat on anymore," Louise recollected. "It seemed like she tried to keep his focus on her, to keep him occupied so he would leave the boys alone. We'd call the law, but it would just cause her to get beat worse."

"Mrs. Moore was such a sweet woman," said Mike Thrower, Louise's son. "She treated all of us like we was hers. She would let Allen and them play ball and things with us in Mr. Dial's pasture when Mr. Moore was gone. If he caught them out of their yard, he would beat Mrs. Moore for it. None of the neighbors would say nothing to him; they were all scared, I guess. We had all seen him in action and was afraid of him."

In the summer of 1970, Gwendolyn's journey to the well was, mercifully, almost done. Pat had not heard from Gwendolyn in several weeks and was worried about her when, shortly after the Fourth of July, she talked Grady, her husband, into going down to Hogansville on a Saturday afternoon to check on her sister. What they encountered was horrific.

Marshall had gone to town when Pat and Grady arrived to find Gwendolyn sitting in a chair, her eyes swollen and her once beautiful hair all but gone, patchy where it had been pulled out by handfuls. Her feet, bruised and swollen, were propped up on a stool. "What on God's earth happened to you?" Pat asked. "Marshall beat me," Gwendolyn whimpered weakly. "What about your feet?" Pat demanded. "He stomped them so I couldn't get out and walk."

About that time, Marshall drove up. Behaving as if nothing were wrong with what Pat and Grady had walked into, after talking a few minutes, he asked Grady to run to town with him, leaving Pat and his kids alone with Gwendolyn and the boys. Gwendolyn asked Pat to help her lie down and sleep on the couch for a few minutes. She said that Marshall was making her stay awake at night while he slept; if he found her asleep, he would beat her again.

Pat cooked supper while Gwendolyn slept on the couch. When she heard the men drive back into the yard, she woke Gwendolyn up. Later that evening, Gwendolyn told Pat that the beatings had gotten worse, but if she tried to get away, Marshall would surely kill her—then who would look after her boys? She begged Pat not to say anything, that it would only make matters worse. Pat left that evening with a terrible sense of impending doom. She knew that Gwendolyn's situation was certainly bound for catastrophe, but she didn't know how to stop the continuous abuse against her sister. She had done all she knew to do, and now her sister was begging her to keep quiet. She told Gwendolyn to call whenever she needed, that she had a place for her and the boys. It was the last time Pat would see Gwendolyn alive.

The next week, Louise called the Hogansville police when Marshall was beating Gwendolyn. When the police arrived, they were taken to the Turners' kitchen, where they could see into the Moores' house next door. Gwendolyn was sitting in a chair in the kitchen. Marshall was circling Gwendolyn in the chair like a cat taunting its prey. Hogansville police officer Norman Smith said in a 2002 interview:

> *We got the call from Junior Turner that Marshall was beating his wife. When we went into the Turners' kitchen, it was dark, allowing us to see right into the room they were in next door. He was walking around her in the chair, and he was saying, "If you bat an eye, I'll slap you out that chair." She must have blinked, because he would knock her out of the chair. He'd reach down and pull her up by her hair and sit her back in the chair again. He'd tell her again not to blink, and then he'd knock her back to the floor. He hit her like that several times. We called the Sheriff's Office and asked if they wanted us to go in the house until they got there. They said no, that deputies would be there shortly and they would handle it. We couldn't stand to watch it anymore, and we went back into the city.*

Later that night, sheriff's deputies went to the Moore house and found Gwendolyn with her head split open from where she had been hit with a bottle. She was taken to the City-County Hospital in LaGrange, where just after midnight on July 28, 1970, she received eight stitches to close the wound to her head. Marshall accompanied her to the hospital. She told the doctor she had fallen on the concrete porch and hit her head. After her treatment, Marshall took her back to her prison and the continuing nightmare from which she could find no escape.

On the evening of August 3, 1970, Gwendolyn expected Marshall to be late getting home from driving for Brown Transport. Earlier that day, she had let the boys go with neighborhood children to the swimming pool in Hogansville. When Marshall arrived home earlier than expected, he found Gwendolyn at home with the baby, Dean, who was now thirteen months old. Upon discovering that Gwendolyn had given the children permission to go to the pool, he flew into a rage and all hell broke loose.

In the 1970s, central air was not common to most houses. The only relief from the oppressive August heat ordinary to the Deep South was to keep all the windows open to catch a cross breeze. The Moore house was situated between the two Turner family homes. The home to the immediate east was that of Junior Turner; his wife, Louise; and Mike, Jennifer and Debbie Thrower, Louise's children from a prior marriage. The house some fifty feet to the west was that of Ms. Chaucie Turner and her sons Danny, Donnie and Ronnie. Danny had been paralyzed in a car accident years before and was confined to wheelchair. Danny had started

Emergency room record, July 27, 1970. *Troup County Archives.*

a gospel singing group, the Danny Turner Singers. In doing so, he had enlisted a young, attractive and recently divorced Priscilla Shepherd as the pianist for the group.

As the events of that August 3 evening began to unfold, Chaucie, Ronnie, Danny and Priscilla were at the house. With the windows open and the proximity of the houses, Ronnie heard the savagery begin to unfold. He went to the corner of their front porch, where he had a direct view into the Moores' home. Ronnie could hear Marshall's booming voice yelling as he methodically beat Gwendolyn into unconsciousness. Ronnie said that he called out to his mother to come outside, that he thought Marshall was going to kill her this time. Ronnie's mother came to the porch, and after seeing the savagery firsthand, she turned to go back into the house, saying, "I got to call the law." She was met at the door by Priscilla, who Ronnie said told his mother, "Now Chaucie, that's their business, and we don't need to get in it; she'll be all right." Three months after Gwendolyn's death, Priscilla would marry Marshall Moore, ensuring that the chance of any justice for Gwendolyn would remain crushed beneath the wheels of the Machine; her father, Robert Shepherd, would see to it.

Ronnie, re-creating the scene years later and shaking his head as tears welled up in his eyes, said, "Clay, I'll never forget it. He had torn her clothes off and was sitting down on her. She was laying on her back, and he'd grab her by her hair and pick her head up, and then he'd knock her head down to the floor with his fist. After a few times, she just went limp, and he was still beating her. Finally, he got up and bent down and started to snatch what I thought was her hair out one at a time. Then I heard him say, 'Now go get you some more stitches, bitch.' Then he just walked off, leaving her on the floor. He walked out of the house and got in his car and left."

"After a few minutes, she began to try to get up," Ronnie recalled. "She crawled over to the bed and used the bedpost to climb to her feet. She was beat pitiful. I'll never forget the sight of that poor woman's bare backside as she tried to pull on a pair of yellow shorts. She felt around and found her white blouse. She struggled and got it pulled on, and the last time I saw her alive, she was stumbling out of the door going toward Mike Thrower's house. Clay, it was just pitiful," Ronnie said as he choked back his tears.

"Ronnie, is that exactly how you remember it? I mean, you just told me what she was wearing, and you saw this one time thirty-three years ago. That's a lot to remember."

"Hell, Clay, that ain't the way I remember it, that's exactly the way it was: I ain't just seen this one time; I've seen it nearly every day for thirty-three years. I'll never forget it, I'll never forget it." And then he added regretfully, "I should have done something to save her."

Gwendolyn left that night and went to Junior Turner's house, begging for help. The Turner kids, alone by themselves, hid their neighbor in the crawlspace under the house as their parents had done in the past. "If he finds me, he'll kill me, and I don't want to die," Gwendolyn moaned pitifully through her tears and the blood. "I got to get help for me and my babies."

Mike Thrower, Louise's son, went under the house to check on Mrs. Moore a short time later. "She was hurt bad," he recalled. "It looked like one eye was completely shut and the other one was just barely open. She started to talk like she was confused. I guess she was just beat senseless. I told her that when Junior and Mama got home, they would take her to get help."

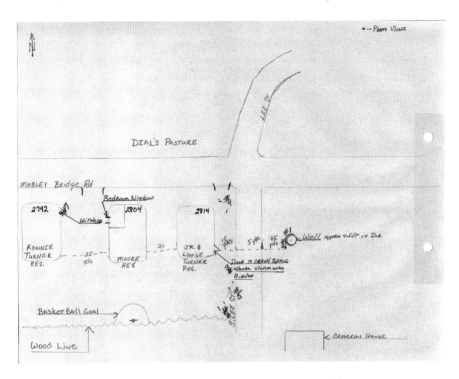

Above: Diagram showing relevance of locations to witness statements and general topography of the crime scene. *Author's collection.*

Left: View down into the abandoned well where Gwendolyn's body was found. *Author's collection.*

From the well to Junior Turner's crawlspace door. The trees and undergrowth did not exist in 1970. *Author's collection.*

That, however, was not meant to be, for when Junior returned home from picking Mrs. Turner up from work, he was told of Gwendolyn's situation. He searched throughout the forbidding crawlspace darkness beneath the house. The piercing beam of his flashlight found only an empty spot where her battered body had been.

August 4, 1970, dawned with the air thick and close. Junior arose early, worrying about what had happened to Gwendolyn. Maybe she had gone home, or maybe she had walked to town for help. He could see activity in the Moore house, but there was no sign of Gwendolyn—that was totally out of character.

This image shows the spatial relationship between Junior Turner's residence and the Moore residence. *Author's collection.*

Fearing the worst, Junior Turner sent the kids out to scour the yard and surroundings in case his neighbor was hurt so badly she couldn't get back to the house. A few minutes passed, and Jennifer, the second oldest, came running into the house screaming, "Come quick, I can see Gwen's in the old well. I think she's dead."

Junior ran out the door and across the yard to the old homeplace next door. At the bottom of the well, he could see Gwendolyn, her body slumped over in a crouched position as if she were praying. As he gazed in horror at the bottom of the forbidding hole, he couldn't help but wonder why it had to come to this for her poor soul to find peace. Little did Junior

This image shows the view Ronnie Turner had into the Moores' bedroom window on August 3, 1970. The trees and vegetation were not present at the time. *Author's collection.*

Turner know that what he believed to be peace for Gwendolyn was only the beginning of anguished cries to be heard decades later demanding justice from the well.

EVERY CRIME HAS ITS MOTIVE

Since the beginning of recorded history, men and women have murdered and been murdered—a sad statement about the inhumanity of our species. The motives for murder are as many and varied as the sick individuals who commit these crimes: hatred, jealousy, greed, revenge, passion and the list goes on. All are reasons that in a twisted mind justify the taking of the life of another.

Gwendolyn Moore endured a life of tyranny and brutality for some fifteen years, all while bearing four children. It was a life that transformed her from an attractive, vibrant young woman into a battered hermit living in a constant state of fear and intimidation. This sad change resulted in her becoming undesirable to Marshall, who by now saw her as his slave and a hindrance to the life he wanted to live.

Marshall had developed a reputation as a tough guy and a bully in certain circles. He could be found in the beer joints and clubs in Troup County, where he would strike up relationships with the people who controlled the underground vices that thrived in the county. Marshall was a truck driver by trade and operated a small freight terminal for Brown Transportation. Brown contracted with Milliken Inc., one of the nation's largest manufacturers of textiles and carpeting. It would be discovered that Milliken Inc. was the victim of a tremendous amount of product theft through a conspiracy of some its employees and certain shipping company employees. After Gwendolyn's death, this situation would come to light, ultimately resulting in some employees being fired and some prosecuted for their actions. Through his association with both, Marshall would be found to be a valuable asset to the guys who ran the Machine. He was much too valuable to let the "Gwendolyn Incident" get in the way of business.

One of those men was Robert Shepherd, owner of the Eagle's Club, whom Marshall befriended. Through Shepherd, Marshall would become known as a useful tool for intimidation as well as income. Marshall reveled in his newfound role as a bad boy, and often, according to Gwendolyn's family members, he bragged that he had connections and could get away with pretty much anything in Troup County. He thoroughly enjoyed rubbing elbows with the county's criminal elite, as well as the elevated status he felt those shady associations brought him.

Robert Shepherd's father, Wallace Shepherd, through the façade of his legitimate businesses, wielded the political clout to ensure protection for his son's illegitimate interests and those of his associates. Robert always relied on his father for guidance and support.

Robert had two daughters, Phyllis and Priscilla; he also raised a stepdaughter, Dell Kuhlman. Dell, a devout Christian, laughingly said that Robert had taught her how to shoot dice and play poker as a child: "I didn't know any better back then." After divorcing the girls' mother, Robert was never close to Phyllis. He did, however, cultivate a close relationship with his other daughter, Priscilla.

Priscilla was a very attractive woman. She filed for divorce from her high school sweetheart husband, Wayne Helms, in 1969, sometime around when she met Marshall Moore. Priscilla, having been raised under the bad boy influence of her father, found it easy to be attracted to a man like Marshall Moore.

Either by chance or otherwise, she became employed as the pianist for the Danny Turner Singers, which put her in proximity to Marshall. As for the motive that resulted in Gwendolyn's lifeless body ending up in that well, no one can be absolutely sure. Was it blind rage because of the frustration Marshall felt from being trapped in a life he was desperate to get out of? Or was it even more sinister? Could he have been purposefully eliminating what he saw as a stumbling block impeding his starting a new life with someone he desired more?

One has to wonder after seeing the cruelty firsthand and hearing the horror stories of what continually went on in the Moore home from the Turners: why would a woman subject herself to the possibility of the same lifestyle? Only Priscilla Shepherd could answer that question.

Two facts remain certain. According to witnesses, it was Priscilla Shepherd who intervened in Chaucie Turner's attempt to call the police as Gwendolyn was being savagely beaten on the night of her death. Also, Marshall Moore would marry Priscilla Shepherd less than four months after Gwendolyn's lifeless body was found in the well.

Marshall's close ties to the Machine, through the Shepherds, ensured that the investigation into Gwendolyn's death hit a brick wall. Sheriff Bailey would see to that. The death of a helpless nobody woman with no local ties would not be allowed to interfere with the workings of the Machine or the desires of its members. The sheriff would do all he could to stifle the cries for justice from the well.

A RUMBLING FROM THE WELL

I was hoping you might could help me out, Clay. I was told you might remember something about an old murder case a woman called me about."

In 2002, I had been back in police work for a grand total of two weeks and was contemplating the administrative work associated with updating my peace officer certification when Larry Arrington, an investigator with the Troup County Sheriff's Office, called me at the DA's Office on a bright autumn morning in October. I hadn't even had a chance to get my feet wet really and was just settling into my new position as criminal investigator for Pete Skandalakis, district attorney for the Coweta Judicial Circuit, which encompasses five counties in west-central Georgia, when I answered Larry's call.

It was my job to conduct special investigations at the request of the DA, as well as to assist local agencies in whatever way possible on cases in five counties: Carroll, Coweta, Heard, Meriwether and Troup. Part of my job description was to locate and re-interview witnesses on cases presented for prosecution by our police agencies.

"A woman named Leslie Power called and wanted to know some specifics on a death investigation involving her great-aunt, and I can't seem to locate any record of the investigation," Larry said. "It's as if it never happened." This last statement alone was enough to pique my interest.

Larry went on to tell me that the incident occurred in 1970 outside Hogansville, where the woman was found dead in a dry well. Immediately,

I knew, and it wasn't the chill in the air that made me shiver. "It's been a while," I told him, "but I was standing there when she was brought up from that well."

"You've got to be kidding," Larry replied.

"No, I was there with my dad," I explained. "The Sheriff's Office had asked him to come out and take some pictures for them, and I tagged along."

Larry then related to me that Leslie Power had faxed him a copy of a death certificate that raised more questions than provided answers. I told Larry the things I had heard my father say about the case, including his belief that Marshall Moore had murdered his wife and disposed of her body in the well.

Larry asked if I would talk with Ms. Powers. He told me he would fax over a copy of the death certificate and Leslie's phone number. As I waited for Larry to send the information, all thoughts of my peace officer certification disappeared, and my mind drifted back to that summer of 1970. I thought of my father and how profoundly this old case had affected the course of his life. I couldn't help wondering, as I had so many times before, what might have been had my daddy lived.

Death certificates are usually mundane documents. As important as they are, they generally tend to be nondescript to the untrained eye. The cause of death is usually described in medical terms intelligible only to those with at least some degree of medical knowledge. This document, however, was like no other I had seen in the past.

Dr. Joseph Kraftka was the resident pathologist at City-County Hospital in 1970. He was also the county's medical examiner. These two titles did not always go hand in hand, and not all medical examiners were trained in death investigation. Dr. Kraftka was, as most pathologists seemed to be in my experience, a bit eccentric. He drove a bright red Cadillac convertible, and folks who knew him jokingly referred to him as the "Cadillac Kid" or "Doctor Death." He was quite a character, but he was also a gifted pathologist. Thorough and concise, he made it apparent from his entries on Gwendolyn Moore's death certificate that he had strong professional opinions as to the cause and manner of her death.

Under the heading "Manner of Death" was one word: *homicide*. In the block reserved for "Cause of Death," the words were glaring: "pulmonary edema, due to concussion caused by repeated blows to the head."

Dr. Kraftka had been thorough and done his homework. He found that Gwendolyn Moore had been treated at City-County Hospital on July 28 after being hit in the head with a bottle. Her head had been sutured to

Copy of Gwendolyn's original death certificate. *Moore Case File.*

close the wound. He also discovered that Marshall Moore had made a statement that he had "slapped her around" on the night of August 3, 1970. Dr. Kraftka characterized the slapping as being "beaten about the eyes with fists." The evidence as to what this woman had suffered plainly told the awful story. Dr. Kraftka was certain that the woman found in the well had been beaten to death.

It is uncommon to find results of an autopsy so completely outlined on the death certificate. But in doing so, Dr. Kraftka must surely have hoped that his findings would make their way into the hands of some concerned individual who would act on the obvious—someone who would act in a judicious and timely manner.

As I read the report, I recalled Buddy's full-on outrage at the indifference shown toward the death of Gwendolyn Moore. Although I had always been aware of the turmoil he experienced, I was beginning to understand why he had felt the way he did. As I thought of my dad and all that I'd heard of the old case, I became resolved to discover the truth surrounding the death of Gwendolyn Moore.

I called the number I had been given for Leslie Power and was greeted by a well-spoken young lady who seemed somewhat skeptical of my intentions. I told her I had been at the well when her aunt was found, and I shared with her what I believed happened. Leslie was shocked and could not understand why nothing had been done to bring justice in her great-aunt's death.

"I didn't even know Gwen existed," Leslie told me. "Mother and I were cleaning out my grandmother's effects after her death when I came across the death certificate. Mother told me that Gwendolyn was my aunt, her sister, and had died in 1970 under suspicious circumstances—and that the family always believed her husband had killed her, so I felt compelled to find out what really happened. The more I found out from our family, the more I was convinced my grandmother's baby sister was murdered."

Leslie supplied me with names and phone numbers of other relatives with whom I could speak. I promised her that I would do all I could to find the truth about Gwendolyn's death. It was as curious to me as it was to Leslie why her great-aunt's death was never investigated thoroughly. There appeared to be a wealth of evidence that had been totally disregarded. Why was this young woman considered to be of such insignificance that no one would take the time to bring her murderer to justice? In my mind, no one human being is more deserving than another when it comes to finding out the truth.

All I could be sure of was that the flag Dr. Kraftka raised thirty-four years earlier had found the concerned eye of a great-niece who would not rest until she got some answers about her Great-Aunt Gwendolyn's death.

Leslie Power, too, had heard the voice crying out from the well.

Anything but Routine

B y definition, *routine* means "performed as part of a regular procedure rather than for a special reason." Using this word is part of the everyday vernacular for a police officer. "Routine investigation," "routine traffic stop" and "routine patrol" are phrases used to describe the day-to-day aspects of police work. The irony is that a good officer or investigator who falls into the trap of "routine" dooms himself to drown in single-mindedness, a rut that, at best, renders him ineffective and, at worst, makes him a danger to himself and others.

It has always seemed strange to me how a man or woman can be given a badge, a gun and the power to take away the one thing held most precious in our society—a person's freedom—and then be told not to be inquisitive, innovative or resourceful in the plying of that trade, when it is precisely the application of those qualities that makes the officer most effective.

"Son, never get to the point in your life as a peace officer that you handcuff yourself with your own intelligence," Daddy said to me one day while I was riding patrol with him. Attentive to one of his treasured mobile philosophy lessons, I waited for more words of wisdom. "Crime is something that has its own character and circumstance. When you try to make it fit the mold that you want or need for it to, you become a prisoner of your own inability to be flexible and adapt. There are times when the situation has to dictate the course of action, and if you don't go with the flow, you will flounder around until you sink." His plain truth sounded like an odd mixture of Andy Griffith, Bill Gillespie, Charlie Chan and Will Rogers.

Copy of fax from Larry Arrington regarding Gwen's death certificate showing date of October 24, 2002, my father's birthday. *Author's collection.*

Until recently, I did not believe in the supernatural. However, what would come to pass almost a quarter of a century later, I now reason, could only be at the direction of my father and Gwendolyn Moore. Professionally, I no longer wandered aimlessly, for this odyssey would lead me on a path toward resolution. There were too many clues coming from out of the blue to help me rectify a wrong of the highest magnitude. I knew in my gut that I was being guided back into my father's fold.

In late October 2002, I knew that I had to go with the flow until there was resolution, if that were indeed possible. I called on my respected friend Gary Fuller, a retired GBI agent and one of the best investigators I have ever known, who is, in my estimation, above all else, a true peace officer. After hearing my story of how the case came to me and the strength of my feelings about the need to bring justice, Gary offered his advice and a promise to assist me. In the coming months, this pledge of support from my old friend would prove invaluable.

I next contacted Joe Jackson, agent-in-charge of Region Two of the Georgia Bureau of Investigation, and asked for any archived information on the case that Troy Owen had opened so many years ago. Jackson asked if I was sure Owen had been the agent, since he had never heard of an agent by this name. I was sure. Joe promised that he would have the Archive Department research the case and get back in touch with me, but he also told me that he held out little hope for success.

On my first day at the DA's Office, I had the pleasure of meeting Kaye Minchew, director of the Troup County Archives. Over the next several months, she and the archives staff members—Barry Jackson, Lance Jones and Diana Thompson—became tremendous resources to me. I approached Kaye on October 24, 2002, for assistance with my search for background on the case. The archives is the keeper of all historic records for the county, but it had been opened only about ten years after the death of Gwendolyn Moore. Nonetheless, the archives had acquired public records of the county offices dating as far back as possible. This included all records brought forth by area officials at the time.

Fortunately for the case, Kaye Minchew took a deep interest in it. She recalled boxed records stored at the archives dating back to Sheriff Bailey's administration. She also remembered receiving a telephone call from Leslie Power a short time back. Leslie had done her own research, but her initial findings were limited to a few publications and a record of the coroner's request.

Kaye also informed me that the archives had coroners' records from Jack Cleveland's administration as well as all newspaper accounts of the period. All the material was meticulously labeled, and its location in the archives was recorded on their computer database. Physically putting hands on these records was left to the expertise of the staff, a daunting task considering there are literally hundreds of thousands of documents that have been stored. Kaye and her staff seemed to accomplish this undertaking with remarkable efficiency.

As for other records, I knew that Gwendolyn's body had not been brought in through the hospital's emergency room, but instead went straight to the morgue. This meant that a patient's chart, which would have been kept forever, was never created. The records of her final trip to the hospital would be kept only in the Pathology Department (which allowed for the in-house records to be purged at the ten-year mark) and not in Patient Records. This fact caused

Kaye Minchew, director of the Troup County Archives. *Kate Minchew.*

a near fatal blow to the investigation. It would take the divine grace of God and a lot of blood, sweat and tears to obtain the necessary documentation needed to salvage what Sheriff Bailey, and time, had done to the case.

Gwendolyn's death certificate, fortunately, did allude to her injuries that had been treated on the morning of July 28, 1970, at City-County Hospital, where she received stitches in her scalp; this documentation would help substantiate the fact that she was the victim of domestic violence and, if the case were to develop, prove to be highly beneficial. The next step was to prepare an affidavit for a search warrant to obtain the victim's treatment records regarding this incident from West Georgia Medical Center. Judge Quillian Baldwin, Superior Court judge of Troup County, issued a search warrant on that affidavit, and the records of Gwendolyn's treatment were obtained from the hospital.

Due to the fact that I was familiar with all those associated with the case, I was able to develop a list of neighbors who may have been in a position to shed some light on the circumstances of the death of Gwendolyn Moore. Little did I realize at the time just how many people, appalled by the injustice of this case, were ready to shine a piercing beam of truth into the darkness of the well.

HUNTING THE TRAIL

When I was a young boy, my daddy would take me along when he went coon hunting with his buddies. They'd turn the dogs out, and the best of the dogs would go out and begin to circle with their noses to the ground, nostrils flaring, searching for the scent of the track. Like those hunts of my younger years, if the hunt for justice for Gwendolyn was going to get off the ground, I had to find a track.

To begin, I needed to locate written historical accounts of this case in order to move forward. Larry had told me that there were no records of the case from the Bailey administration, but I knew of one person currently on staff with the sheriff's department who had been there from the start; I was sure no one had thought to ask her about it. Joyce Bryan had been the office secretary for Sheriff L.W. Bailey.

Joyce had stayed with the county after Bailey was defeated and moved around within the county government through a series of transfers. The current sheriff, Donnie Turner, had known Joyce for many years, and he also knew that she had a wealth of knowledge about the citizens of Troup County. For this reason, Donnie had requested that she move back to the Sheriff's Office, and she was working as the booking records clerk.

I phoned Joyce and asked her if she remembered the Moore case. Although at first she could not recall the name, once I offered a description of events, she said, "Clay, you're talking about the lady in the well."

"Indeed I am," I said, knowing I had hit pay dirt. "I'm looking into the old case."

"I'm sure glad you are," she said, "I was so mad about the way Bailey handled that case!"

"Are there any records at all on the case?"

"Well, just a few records were boxed and taken to the archives when Gene Jones was elected, but I'm not sure if anything about that case was in there," she answered. "I doubt you'll find anything. You know how Bailey was, but I'll be glad to take a day and help you look."

Joyce also told me about Troy Owen, a close friend and drinking buddy of Bailey's. Owen, a member of the Georgia Bureau of Investigation, lived in LaGrange and had assisted with the case. The two men had a long history dating back to their days with the Georgia Highway Patrol in the 1940s. I thought there might be an outside chance there would be an old case file in the GBI Archives at the headquarters in Atlanta. In the back of my mind, I hoped for and envisioned a few preliminary records about the case the GBI would have required Troy to send in as the investigation was starting up.

Elaine Prescott had worked in pathology at the West Georgia Medical Center for years. If there was anyone in the world who would have an inside track on the location of the original autopsy report and any notes that Dr. Kraftka had made as he worked the case, it would be Elaine. I called the Pathology Department at the hospital and told Elaine what I was hoping she could provide me. My heart sank when she told me that back in the '70s, pathology records were destroyed after ten years. A glimmer of hope arose, however, when she commented that some records had been taken to the hospital archives at the old Coleman Library. She offered to dig through what was there in hope of finding some information that might help the case.

I also mentioned to Elaine that I had a copy of Gwendolyn's death certificate and asked if I could get a pathologist at the hospital to take a gander at it. She advised me to contact Dr. David Martin, head of the Pathology Department; Elaine felt confident that he would help me if he could. Dr. Martin and I met that afternoon.

"It's uncommon for a death certificate to contain the information this one does, Clay," he told me, reaffirming what I had already suspected. "It's as if Dr. Kraftka wanted to make a statement that the family and others would be able to access, as a matter of public record that could not be altered or tampered with in any way."

After our consultation, Dr. Martin said that he would be glad to help me and would testify about the injury causing Gwendolyn's death. He also suggested that I check to see if I could get the State Medical Examiner's

Office involved with the case since it now handled all forensic autopsies for the local hospital, as well as for most counties in the state. Dr. Martin knew that with the case being as old as it was, we would need strong evidence to be able to breathe life back into an investigation.

My next step was to contact people on Leslie's list. The first of these I spoke with was Patricia Terry, Gwendolyn's older sister. Miss Pat, as I came to know her, lived just north of Franklin, Georgia, off Highway 27. When I called Miss Pat and introduced myself, I told her I would like to speak with her about some of the things Leslie had unearthed.

The next morning found me knocking on the door of her neat country home in Heard County. A diminutive lady in her sixties, Miss Pat greeted me at the door and invited me into her living room. My main purpose in meeting with Miss Pat was to gather a sense of how the family felt about restarting the investigation of a case that would open old wounds. At this point, all I had to offer as an impetus was the death certificate and what I personally remembered about the chain of events.

As Miss Pat and I talked, I became extremely aware of her feelings about what had happened to her sister and how the investigation had been handled. She spoke frankly, and I could tell early on that she held out no hope of finding justice for her sister. Pat shared with me stories of Marshall and Gwendolyn's relationship, pointing out that it was abusive from the start. She told me that immediately after their marriage in 1955, there were clear signs of abuse on Gwendolyn: the black eyes, swollen cheeks and missing teeth—all indications of the brutal mistreatment that would continue for the next fifteen years.

At the time of Gwendolyn's death, Pat told me, everyone in the family believed that Marshall killed her, and for some time, they continuously called the Troup County Sheriff's Office to see what progress was being made on the case. "We just expected every day to hear they had arrested him," Pat reflected, "but he had always said he had 'connections' and that he could get away with things."

On that crisp October morning, I listened intently to Miss Pat, overwhelmed as I heard her speak of her baby sister and completely unaware that four hours had passed so quickly. The genuine affection she still felt for Gwendolyn, even after all these years, was extremely evident—in her smiles, in her tears, in her anger that remained over the way Gwendolyn had been forgotten. That day, I came to understand just how greatly the loss of her sister had affected her, as well as how the indifference of the sheriff had added insult to injury.

During the 1970s, the most powerful position in a southern county belonged to the sheriff. In those days, he had control of the criminal justice system; he held authority over the jail and the path for all criminal cases as they moved forward toward court dates. If, for whatever reason, the sheriff wanted a case to disappear, it would never be seen again. If what Miss Pat told me was correct, it appeared that was exactly what had happened to the case of Gwendolyn Moore.

"We were just poor, common folks, and we didn't know anything about most things like this," Pat told me, the pain of three decades still thick in her voice. "We were at the mercy of the system. All we knew to do was to call and ask. Everyone in our family was scared of Marshall; he was such a mean man. The longer this went on, the more we thought maybe he did have some type of influence, and that gave us all the more reason to fear him. Maybe if we had lived in Troup County, things would have been different, but it was clear they didn't care about Gwendolyn or us."

As she painted a vivid and disturbing picture for me about Gwendolyn's hellish existence, if I had not known before, I began to realize just how great an injustice this meek, sweet woman had suffered. It was there in Miss Pat's homey living room that I fully understood that if I were ever to discover the truth about this ugly situation, I would have to learn to listen for the guiding voices from the well.

Out of Sight but Never Out of Mind

Ronnie, it's not that I doubt what you are saying, but it has been thirty-two years since you saw this. How can you remember all the minute details of what she wore and exactly what had happened?"

I was genuinely concerned during my interview with Ronnie Turner, who in 1970 was Gwendolyn Moore's next-door neighbor. Ronnie looked at me, his eyes weary with the weight of years past, and with that direct eye-to-eye contact, he smoothed a salve over my concerns.

"Clay," he said, resolutely, "I didn't just see it thirty-two years ago. I've seen it nearly every day for thirty-two years. I'll never forget it. I'll never, ever forget it. You just don't know how many times I've wished I could. If I could have just done something more, maybe it would have ended up different, but I guess I'll never know."

At the young age of fifteen, Ronnie Turner was friend and playmate to the Moore brothers, especially Allen. He was also witness to three years of nonstop brutality that Marshall Moore inflicted on his family, the incessant cruelty that occurred from the first day the Moores moved in to the house next door. Ronnie had seen Gwendolyn take beatings on a regular basis. He had lost count of the times he had seen her with her eyes blackened and lips swollen to twice their size. He had seen the boys whipped unmercifully at the whim of their tyrannical father.

"There were a lot of times that I would walk down to Mr. Red Barnes's store with Allen to get milk, bread or some other grocery staple for the family because Mrs. Moore would be too embarrassed to be seen all beat up,"

Ronnie recalled. "The boys and Mrs. Moore were scared to death of him. If he came home and the boys were with us in Mr. Dial's pasture playing ball, they would get beat, and Mrs. Moore would get it too for letting them go. He'd beat them for just not being in the yard. He was the meanest man I've ever known. We was all terrified of him. Hell, the whole neighborhood was."

"Mrs. Moore was a sweet woman, always smiling when it was just her and us kids," Ronnie continued. "She was just a kind soul. When we was in the yard playing with the black kids down the road, she'd fix us ice water or tea and treated us all like we was hers. I guess that's one reason I could never get over the things I had seen done to her. She was a little, bitty woman, not over five feet tall, and he was a big strong man. I never once seen her raise her hands to defend herself."

Having grown up with the Turner boys, I knew they were the Moores' neighbors at the time of Gwendolyn's death. Ronnie's brother, Donnie, was still living in Hogansville with his aunt. I made a call to him and told him that I was looking into Mrs. Moore's death. Donnie told me that he had seen Gwendolyn and the children beaten on numerous occasions, just as Ronnie had. But on the night Gwendolyn died, Donnie and Ronnie had both seen Marshall beat her more brutally than in the past and leave her unconscious. Ronnie was currently living in the Carrollton area. Donnie said he would have his brother call me. Two days later, the phone rang at my home. It was Ronnie.

"What's up, Doc? This is Tex."

Tex was the name hung on Ronnie many years ago by his friends, and he was stuck with it for the rest of his life. Ronnie and I discussed old times for a while and the fun times we had had together as young boys. We laughed and reminisced for a bit before I brought up the subject of Gwendolyn Moore. His voice tensed and changed significantly from the friendly façade of small talk to a subject from a sweltering August night three decades ago that continued to torment him on a daily basis.

Ronnie recalled that he was at his house when Marshall arrived home on that fateful night. At first, nothing seemed out of the ordinary, but within a few minutes, all hell broke loose. Ronnie told me that he could hear Marshall cursing, and he could hear other loud sounds, as if someone was hitting the walls of the Moore house with an object. Ronnie went to his front porch and looked across the yard toward the Moore house, a scant seventy-five feet or so away from his home.

It was oppressively hot in west-central Georgia on August 3, 1970. Air conditioning was a luxury reserved for only the most affluent, and that did not include those who dwelled in shotgun houses along Mobley Bridge Road. The shotgun houses were narrow and rectangular, usually no more than about twenty feet wide, with rooms arranged one behind the other and doors at each end of the house. These long, skinny, compact, wood-frame structures were named such from the notion of firing birdshot through the front door and out the rear door without touching a wall. Each house had large, high windows that, when open, helped circulate the air in the sweltering Georgia summertime heat. It was through these large portals that Ronnie Turner saw the vivid images that would follow him the rest of his life.

RATIONALIZATION

A Pitiful Excuse

Defense mechanisms come to the surface in most human beings when they are confronted or feel the perception of a threat. These unconscious psychological processes can reduce anxiety arising from unacceptable or potentially harmful stimuli. One of these traits of defense is rationalization, the ability of a person to justify his mistakes, thereby allowing him to shed guilt he should rightfully bear for his actions. Every "normal" human being exhibits these traits to some degree, but psychopathic and sociopathic individuals—such as serial killers, sex offenders and batterers—demonstrate them to an extreme degree.

This cowardly method of dodging responsibility was evident among many of the principals associated with the Gwendolyn Moore case. Whether out of fear, frustration or indifference, people who could have made a difference stood by and allowed the tragic chain of events to continue and progress into one of the greatest failures imaginable—not only of the criminal justice system but of society as a whole.

Many of those involved offered the excuse that it was a different time, with different values, and that all these years later, the rehashing of the case would be an ill wind that would blow no good. The simple truth is this: it was a monumental wrong in 1970 and remains a monumental wrong today.

Gwendolyn Moore deserved the justice that was denied her in 1970. With the help of good people who were never able to rationalize away what had happened to this woman, it became possible to determine the truth and set the record straight. The fact that Gwendolyn's killer might go to his grave without having to admit to and pay for his unspeakable crime made my blood run cold. Over the many years that had passed since the murder, it seemed as if Marshall Moore had convinced himself that his actions could not have been so terrible since he never suffered any consequences for them.

In the first interview I conducted with Marshall, I was repulsed by his words: "Clay, I don't want to talk about my children's mother, but she was just a drunk."

Often, by unknowingly admitting wrongdoing, the perpetrator of a crime will share justification for his actions. Moore was a textbook case.

Debbie Thrower, Junior Turner's sixteen-year-old stepdaughter, was at home the night Gwendolyn, battered and scarred beyond recognition, begged for help at the Turners' back door. Debbie was home with her fourteen-year-old brother, Mike, and her two younger sisters, Jennifer and Angel. Debbie, like all the neighbors, was scared to death of Marshall Moore. When she saw the condition Gwendolyn was in, she quickly told her to go hide under the house in the crawlspace, just like her mother had Gwendolyn do in the past.

As Gwendolyn was making her way under the house, Randal Williamson, Debbie's boyfriend, drove into the Turners' yard. He saw Gwendolyn and spoke with her. "Her eyes were just slits," Randall recalled. "I don't know how she could still see. She was beat just awful. She asked if I would take her for help, but I didn't want to have trouble with her husband, so I told her to go under the house and hide and that we'd do something after Louise got home from work."

By then, it was around ten o'clock. Mike went under the house to check on Gwendolyn and gave this account: "She was propped up on the heater. Her face was covered with blood, and one eye was swelled shut; the other was swollen nearly as bad. There was a cut on her head that was bleeding badly, and her lips were twice the size they should have been and were bleeding too. She told me she had to get help. She asked if I thought she could walk to town to the police station. I told her about an old logging road that would take her through the woods and bring her back out on Mobley Bridge Road, away from the house where Marshall couldn't see her."

By now, Marshall had become wildly frantic. When he had returned home from retrieving the boys at the pool, he found that Gwendolyn had recovered enough to flee. He could ill afford for her to be seen running around the neighborhood in the condition she was in. Allen recalled that when the boys returned home with their father to find their mother gone, Marshall immediately went outside to look for her. He was handling himself in a hurried, chaotic way, shouting orders to the boys. Taking Allen with him, Marshall told Allen to go over to the Turners' house to see if his mother was hiding there.

At the Turners' house, Mike told Allen that his mother was in the crawlspace under the house. Allen found her cringing in the darkness, alert to every movement and sound yet unable to move from her hiding place. His mother's last words to him would echo in his mind forever: "I'm going to get help. Take care of Dean 'til I get back. Don't tell your daddy where I am, or he'll kill me. I don't want to die. I love you, son."

Allen emerged from under the neighbor's house to spot his father searching for Gwendolyn with a flashlight at the wood line behind the row of shotgun houses. Allen did as his mother had instructed him; he told his father he couldn't find her. Frightened and not sure what to do other than exactly what his mother had said, Allen returned to his home to look after his baby brother. The thought of his mother's last hours, of her cowering in that dark, damp, filthy crawlspace, would haunt him for the rest of his days.

My initial attempt to find the documentation I so desperately needed was going nowhere fast. Unless I was able to locate at least a starting point to the old investigation, my efforts were apt to stop dead in the water. What I could determine from my early interviews was that a tremendous injustice might very well go uncorrected if I was unable to secure absolute evidence worth enough to take the case to trial.

In mid-November, I received a call from Chris Hosey, assistant GBI agent-in-charge of our region. Hosey provided me with some welcome news: intelligence had found the old case file submitted by Troy Owen. I wasted no time in driving to the GBI offices in nearby Greenville to retrieve the precious file; on the drive back, my impatience with having to wait to return to my office in LaGrange to read it won. I pulled off to the side of Greenville Road with the anticipation of a kid at Christmas and read the entire file within five minutes.

From cover to cover, the file consisted of only four pages, with only one of these pages containing interviews. The summary page, dated February 7, 1971, read, "After an intensive investigation, it is the opinion of this investigator, that this case should be closed." That was all. Cut and dried.

One of the first statements that caught my attention was that of Gwendolyn's son Allen. He stated, "Daddy killed my mama and threw her in that well. And if he finds out I'm telling you this, he'll kill me too."

Not included in the file was an autopsy report or any scientific findings—items that would normally be included in any major case file. Such an

Coroner's report, 1970. *Troup County Archives.*

overt attempt to do nothing seemed unimaginable. The apparent lack of investigation into the crime perpetrated against Gwendolyn Moore was the product of the Troup County Machine. Officials chose to ignore the obvious and instead created unlikely possibilities that could justify their indifferent inaction.

After receiving the report, I took my interviews, along with the old case file, to my boss, D.A. Pete Skandalakis. After hearing my theory on what had happened, Pete seemed a bit more interested in the case. "Keep digging, you might have something," he said. "But we've still got a long way to go to make this thing fly. I want you to pull all you can together and let Lynda look at it and see what she thinks, then we'll talk again."

Having only been in the office just a little more than a month, I did not know Lynda Caldwell very well. I did know that she was regarded as a good lawyer and competent prosecutor. When I interviewed for the job of chief investigator, I had done so with Lynda, whose title was senior assistant

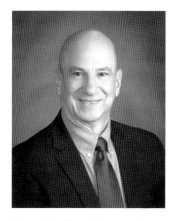

Peter John (Pete) Skandalakis, district attorney for the Coweta Judicial Circuit. *Peter John Skandalakis.*

Lynda Caldwell, assistant district attorney. *Lynda Caldwell.*

district attorney in the Troup County Office of the Coweta Judicial Court.

My first opportunity to work closely with Lynda was on the Moore case. Pleasant and professional, Lynda is what would be called direct. She says what she means and means what she says, a rare and refreshing trait in the legal world. People who don't know her might be intimidated by her straightforwardness. Working in the coming months with her on this case and others, I would come to respect her not only as an exceptional lawyer and prosecutor but also as a justice-seeking individual and friend.

Lynda was raised in Ohio, far removed from the good ol' boy network of Sheriff Bailey and the Boys. I hoped that she would be able to understand how corrupt the system here used to be and that the forebears of our noble professions would stop at nothing when it came to their own desires and conspiracies to justify murder.

When speaking with Pete Skandalakis initially, I told him all I knew of the case, including the history of domestic violence, corruption and the cover-up. As I was ranting on about all the injustices in the case, Pete spoke his usual words of wisdom. "As awful as the case is, it's a very simple case also," he said. "All we have to do is make the case that she died as a result of his actions. But to do that, the testimony of the pathologist is absolutely critical. No testimony as to the cause of death…no case."

With the original autopsy report unavailable to us, we had only the death certificate to establish the actual cause of death. As specific as it was, it was short of being a complete autopsy report that would survive as primary evidence at trial. With Dr. Kraftka having passed away many years earlier, I would have to resort to extreme measures in order to breathe life back into the case. We had to have more than a faint voice crying out for justice from the darkness of the well.

Enter the Doctor of Death

In March 2003, I contacted Georgia's chief medical examiner, Dr. Kris Sperry. Recognized as one of the leading forensic pathologists in the country, Dr. Sperry not only testifies in Georgia but also serves as an expert in the field of forensic pathology in cases throughout the country.

To say that Dr. Sperry is a busy man is to put it mildly. Fortunately, he has one of the most efficient and capable assistants in Mrs. Jimmie Bailey. While Dr. Sperry harbors the forensic knowledge, Mrs. Bailey protects him like a lioness while keeping him on task and on schedule as he testifies throughout the state and across the nation. My first hurdle was to make a case to Mrs. Bailey as to why I needed an audience with her boss.

I told Mrs. Bailey about the death certificate and the statements of pertinent witnesses, about the lost autopsy report and how we would be dead in the water without it unless I was able to find a pathologist to testify as to the cause of death. Mrs. Bailey asked me to fax the death certificate directly to her, and she promised she would show it to Dr. Sperry. She assured me that she would call back within a day or two to give me the verdict.

I was as nervous as a long-tailed cat in a room full of rocking chairs as the minutes ticked by over the next few days. Near the end of the first week in November, Mrs. Bailey called. "Dr. Sperry says he would like to speak with you about your case," she said. "Can you bring your complete file to his office on the 18th at ten in the morning? He will talk with you then."

With my foot in the door, I could only bide my time until we met and hope that I would be able to convince Dr. Sperry of the merits of my case. One thing was certain: at the time, Kris Sperry's professional opinion carried great weight in the world of forensic science; his reputation was stellar, and he would only testify to what he believed to be the truth. It was this maxim by which he lived that made him one of the most sought-after experts in forensic pathology. He was nationally renowned as a man who displays no qualms about testifying on behalf of a defendant when the evidence points toward innocence. Opinion as to what happened to Gwendolyn would mean nothing to him; only evidence would be taken into account.

I would spend several sleepless nights between the first week of November and the eighteenth as I awaited this crucial intersection in the road to justice for Gwendolyn. The appointed hour finally came, and with great anticipation, I made the drive to the Georgia Bureau of Investigation office in Atlanta. Located on Panthersville Road, GBI headquarters consists of a sprawling complex just off Interstate 285 in DeKalb County. The crime lab itself is a division of the Georgia Bureau of Investigation. I went directly to the Medical Examiner's Office and located Mrs. Bailey.

After what felt like hours (but was actually a brief wait), a rather nondescript man with large wire-rimmed glasses came to meet me. This was Dr. Sperry, and I followed him into his lair. Located in the center of an expansive office, his desk was covered with papers, books, case files and numerous other items. His walls were lined with bookcases containing volume after volume relevant to the plying of his trade. Humorous caricatures and figures adorned his desk and covered the remaining spaces on his walls. I stood in the middle of Dr. Sperry's self-made chaotic organization. The room was that of a cluttered genius, one who attempted to create as much levity and lightheartedness as possible in the grim reality of his profession.

Sometimes a person's appearance doesn't match what you have imagined by speaking with him over the phone. Gary Fuller had told me I would be surprised when I met Dr. Sperry; Gary was correct. I had fully expected to meet a reserved funeral director type, a conservative stuffed shirt who would seek to impress me with his vast knowledge. The man I had followed into the office was in no way anything like I had visualized.

Relatively short and stocky, Kris Sperry appeared to be in his mid-forties. Thick glasses accented his prematurely balding head, and he sported quite elaborate tattoos on each of his arms beneath the sleeves of the University of Georgia football jersey he wore. Clad in a pair of jeans and a pair of old white tennis shoes, it was apparent that Kris Sperry didn't try to impress anyone. After only a few minutes with him, it became obvious that he had no reason to do so. Kris Sperry was all about substance.

He asked to see my file. As we spoke of the case, Kris located the items he felt would be most relevant to his opinion: the death certificate, statements by Ronnie Turner and Allen Moore, the old hospital records of prior treatment and Coroner Jack Cleveland's report.

I never got the chance to begin my well-rehearsed narrative because every time I would think about bringing up a point of relevance, Kris would ask the very question I was about to address. As we spoke, I acquired a tremendous respect for Dr. Kris Sperry. He was inquisitive about not only the criminal aspects of the case but also the human results that arose from it. From my brief time with him, I became confident that whatever his decision was—win, lose or draw—Dr. Sperry would render his decision based solely on the merits of the evidence before him.

Once he had pored over the file, asking and finding answers to the necessary questions, Dr. Sperry leaned back in his chair. He set the file on his lap and squinted slightly. "The death certificate is certainly detailed," he said. "It is obvious that Dr. Kraftka was making a strong statement. A strong case can be made as to the cause of death even with the absence of a pathology report. I certainly would like for you to continue to seek that report. I can testify that the injuries described in the death certificate would be consistent with statements of the witnesses, and that would support the findings on the death certificate. Again, even in the absence of anything further, I can agree with the cause of death and the fact that it was a homicide."

I was ecstatic! For the moment, the one hurdle that could not be avoided had been cleared, or so it seemed. Dr. Sperry instructed me to continue with the investigation and, above all else, seek all documentation having to do with the pathologist's report and notes from the autopsy itself.

With Dr. Sperry on board, I could see the light at the end of this tunnel. What I did not foresee was that this light was affixed to an oncoming locomotive. The journey that I had anticipated coming to an end was only just beginning.

ONE STEP FORWARD
AND TWO STEPS BACK

A few days after my meeting with Dr. Sperry, I was still on cloud nine. My case file was growing, and I was becoming so involved in circumstances surrounding the case that I couldn't see the reality of my situation. Due to its age, this case was a mountain—not completely insurmountable but, at the very least, a once-in-a-lifetime challenge. So far, things had come easily, perhaps an omen of more challenging times to come.

Late November found me chomping at the bit to get the old case ready to present to the grand jury. Lynda already had a full caseload, and I had not yet come to grips with the demands on the assistant DAs. It was unfathomable to me why she couldn't just drop the hundred or so cases with which she was dealing in order to fast-track my million-to-one long shot.

Long-suffering and patient with my impetuous nature, Lynda finally told me that she and her husband, Mike, a career police officer himself, would be going on a trip out of town for Thanksgiving. She assured me that she would carefully read my case file while she was gone and decide if we had enough to pursue an indictment.

That holiday was excruciatingly long for me, and my mind raced with thoughts of why or why not she would proceed as I waited for yet another verdict on the old case. Lynda appeared in my office the following week.

"Clay, I read your case," she said. Her voice was riddled with emotion. "I didn't realize just how brutal this case was. If it continues to come together, we're going to convict him. He's not going to get away with this." The hard-nosed assistant district attorney had tears in her eyes. Over the next few months, I would bear witness to just how dedicated and determined Lynda was to make sure that justice prevailed for Gwendolyn Moore.

In mid-December, I collected some DNA evidence in a child molestation case. I took the evidence to the crime lab, where I left it with Dawn Pierce, an evidence technician in the forensic biology section of the lab. The few times I had dealt with Dawn, she had proven to be helpful and extremely responsive. In passing, I mentioned the old case to her and that I had hit a wall with regard to finding old reports in the archives of the crime lab. Dawn pointed me to the records section and told me to speak with Diane Ennis, hinting to me that my having been successful in generating more interest in the old case might justify another look for documentation.

Ms. Ennis was receptive to my renewed inquiries. We had searched before by the victim's name only, as the original case file had not listed any suspects. Because the case took place long before the advent of the computer, all records of this age were hard copy and had been transferred to microfilm to reduce the avalanche of papers. Unless you knew the exact specifics of how they had been filed, finding the record you needed was somewhat of a lost cause. There was, however, one avenue Ms. Ennis felt had not been completely explored: she suggested we cross-reference the old GBI case file to the crime lab case number. We knew that at the time the case was opened, all medical examiner's cases were submitted to the crime lab along with autopsy results and tissue samples for examination and toxicology testing. The records should be there; we just needed to determine where to look.

Armed with the old case number, Diane gave it one more shot by crossing the original case number to the crime lab file number. To our amazement and delight, there on the microfiche was Dr. Kraftka's autopsy report, submitted in 1970. Finding this record at last was a major coup.

At first glance, the autopsy report seemed consistent with the opinion stated on the death certificate. Also present was a report of the absence of poisonous gases in the well, along with the toxicology results from the tissue samples submitted. This finding further supported the theory of purposeful cover-up; these reports would not have been left out of a GBI case file inadvertently. The result was a defining moment in making the case for murder.

I was again bolstered by a wave of euphoria. The report seemed to reiterate the concussion diagnosis, and to the unknowing eye, all seemed to be falling right into place. I immediately carried the report to Forensic Pathology and gave it to Mrs. Bailey to pass on to Dr. Sperry, who was in Savannah that day testifying in court.

FORM C. L. 1

THIS FORM TO BE MADE
IN TRIPLICATE

**STATE OF GEORGIA
DEPARTMENT OF PUBLIC SAFETY
CRIME LABORATORY**
GEORGIA BUREAU OF INVESTIGATION
BOX 1456, ATLANTA, GEORGIA

RECORD OF MEDICAL EXAMINER 70-8342

C-70-15
CITY Hogansville _____ COUNTY Troup _____

NOTIFIED BY Coroner Cleaveland _____ HOUR 11:15A. M. DATE 4 August 70

OFFICERS ASSIGNED TO CASE Deputy Sheriff L.W. Webb; Carl Hart; Coroner Cleaveland

OFFICERS EMPLOYED BY Troup County

NAME OF DECEASED MOORE, Gwendolyn (McDaniel) _____ AGE 30 SEX Female RACE Wh HEIGHT 61' WEIGHT

RESIDENCE OF DECEASED Route 2, Hogansville, Mobley Bridge Road.

TIME OF DEATH: HOUR Est. 9P.M. DATE 3 August 70 PLACE OF DEATH Undetermined as yet.
Undetermined as yet.

MANNER OF DEATH: HOMICIDE _____ JUSTIFIABLE _____ ACCIDENTAL _____ SUICIDE _____ NATURAL _____

TIME OF 9:00 P. M. DATE 3 August 70 PLACE OF Undetermined.

METHOD OF Not yet known.

BODY REMOVED FROM Old abandoned deep surface well. REMOVED BY McKibben

DATE RECEIVED AT FUNERAL HOME: 4 August 70 _____ HOUR 4:30 P. M.

NAME OF FUNERAL HOME McKibben

AUTOPSY AUTHORIZED BY Coroner.

PRESENT AT AUTOPSY Medical Examiner.

BODY IDENTIFIED BY Brother.

PHOTOGRAPHS BY Deputy Sheriffs and Medical Examiner.

DATE AUTOPSIED: HOUR 1:00 P.M. DATE 4 August 70 _____ PERFORMED BY Dr. Joseph F. Krafka, M.D.

ACCUSED Undetermined.

NOTE: A COPY OF THIS RECORD SHALL BE SENT TO:

SOLICITOR GENERAL _____ (full report will follow)

CORONER Cleaveland.

OFFICER Sheriff L.W. Bailey.

CAUSE OF DEATH 1. Pulmonary edema.
2. Petechial brain hemorrhages.

EVIDENCE SUBMITTED TO LABORATORY 1. Blood for alcohol, Darvon, Monoxide.
2. Kidney, brain. for toxicology.

DO NOT FILL IN THIS PART OF FORM
(FOR CRIME LABORATORY USE ONLY)

DATE _____ 19

APPROVED _____
(LABORATORY)

DATE 4 August 70 _____ 19 70

SIGNED _____ M.D.

(Cont'd.)

DO NOT FILL IN THIS PART OF FORM
(FOR CRIME LABORATORY USE ONLY)

DATE 1-22-71 _____ 19

APPROVED _____
(LABORATORY)

DATE November 12, 1970 _____ 19

SIGNED Robert R. Sti _____ M.D.
(APPROVED PATHOLOGIST)

(USE ADDITIONAL SHEETS IF NECESSARY)
Robert R. Stivers, M. D.

Original medical examiner's report, 1970. *GBI Crime Laboratory.*

I left Atlanta that afternoon feeling bulletproof, almost intoxicated with all the positive results. I swaggered into the District Attorney's Office and told Patty Smith, one of our administrative assistants, of my great discovery. Patty had been keeping up with the development of the case and was thrilled at my obvious progress. Jeanie Henderson, who was working in the office on a temporary basis, had been helping me with the transcription of all the witness statements. Both she and Patty had become as determined about gaining justice for Gwendolyn as I had.

Once, long ago, my daddy had told me, "Son, an investigation is a long lane that never turns. You may have to backtrack and regroup, but you've got to press forward. When every little pitfall knocks you down, you just have to dust yourself off and keep going. Eventually you'll get a break."

I could see my daddy, with his boyish grin, stopping to laugh at this point in his lecture. "Just remember, boy," he'd continue, "in life, whatever be your goal, keep your eye on the doughnut and not on the hole!" Recalling these bits of jovial advice from my father would get me through what was to be some rough sledding ahead.

It soon became apparent to me that the case I had wanted so badly to present to the grand jury in February wasn't going to be ready; there was still much work to be done. I contacted Allen and Pat to let them know that we would not make the February term but that we would shoot for May instead. They were understanding and not one bit critical of the decision, but I knew how badly they wanted to proceed and I was just as disappointed as they were.

In late March, Lynda met again with Dr. Sperry. At this meeting, Dr. Sperry utilized the old catchphrase, "Houston, we have a problem," as he pointed out that the death certificate showed the pathological conclusions of Dr. Kraftka and that if there had been no changes in the findings, he could have wholeheartedly supported those conclusions. However, the items that were missing were forensic findings, those very items on which Dr. Kraftka had based his own deductions.

In the autopsy report, Dr. Kraftka indicated the presence of petechial hemorrhage of the brain. Petechial hemorrhages are minute hemorrhages of cellular material caused by anaerobic metabolism, meaning without oxygen. Cells within the body derive oxygen from the blood; without that oxygen, the cells will rupture. This causes small hemorrhages that are most noticeable in the eyes and facial features of the victim. This condition is commonly found in victims of traumatic asphyxia. This was not totally consistent with the findings of concussion due to blows to the head, presenting another factor that, without further explanation, muddied the water.

And where did that leave us? Simple. Dr. Sperry needed to see the body.

"Exhumation of the body is no guarantee, perhaps even a long shot at best, Clay," he said. "But with the questions raised by the autopsy report, I cannot render an opinion as to cause of death without a second autopsy, and possibly not even then. The injuries described are soft tissue injuries, and evidence of those is going to be long gone. There is a chance that we could find something in the skull or skeleton that would support a cause of death and reconcile the death certificate to the autopsy report."

Dr. Sperry did not hold out much hope, it appeared. Lynda and I were devastated. After discussing this turn of events with Pete, Lynda and I wanted to pursue the second autopsy, but first we had to present this to the family. Ultimately, it would have to be their decision if we were to proceed.

IN UNITY THERE IS STRENGTH

P ete had Phyllis Williams, one of our victims' advocates, arrange a meeting with all concerned family members in late March 2003. The purpose of the meeting was to advise the family of our progress and the obstacles that we still faced, as well as to gather their input as to their desire to pursue the case. We were to meet in an upstairs conference room in the Troup County Administration Building. Although I had not met them all, I had spoken to each member at one time or another, and I was looking forward to seeing all the family together. At the same time, I was apprehensive about advising them of the need for an exhumation. After all we had been through together, I just was not sure what their reaction would be. I had already broken one of the first rules of investigation, which was never to become emotionally involved in a case. I confess, at this point, that I felt as if I were a part of the family. Cold cases, on the other hand, present somewhat of a different animal; for the most part, they have been lying fallow for years. They present a rather hopeless situation; without shouldering some of the baggage, the outrage and feelings of abandonment and victimization, you would simply do what everyone in the past had done: give up. I was all in.

Each family member had honored me not only by opening up to me but also by showing me his or her own soul, allowing me to be a part of the joys and tragedies of their family for three generations; because we had built a trust-based friendship, the last thing I wanted to do was to hand them another disappointment.

I had promised them that I would do all I could to find justice for Gwendolyn and for the family. I now feared that I might have been too optimistic in my assurances. If this setback devastated them enough, the family might decide that this was just a wild goose chase. I had certainly reopened a lot of old wounds for some good and innocent people.

I credit my father with many things, but on that mild Friday morning in March 2003, it was my mother who came to mind.

Doris Bryant was a devoted wife and mother. Although that sounds a bit cliché, she was simply dedicated to making sure we were safe and content in life. Doris had her quirks, but she was a wonderful mother—sometimes a bit overbearing and overprotective, but only out of the intense love she had for us. She worked every day of her life and wanted no more than success and happiness for her family, the same things that Gwendolyn wanted for hers. It was my mother who taught me a strong work ethic, the meaning of sacrifice and a sense of family.

Because Gwendolyn's family had, to some degree, adopted me into their fold, I feared that they would think the trust they had put in me had been betrayed; I feared they might view me as the one responsible for their pain revisited.

As I sat in my office awaiting the arrival of the family, thoughts of my mother were incredibly strong and clear. It was if she were speaking to me, quoting her favorite prayer, "God, grant me the serenity to accept the things I cannot change, the courage to change the things I can, and the wisdom to know the difference." As I reflected on that prayer, the tremendous anxiety I brought with me to that meeting simply evaporated. I knew that it was in the hands of a higher authority, and I had faith that things would work out as they should.

Meeting with me that morning were my old friend and mentor Gary Fuller; Jeff Cook, the Troup County coroner; Phyllis; Lynda; Pete; and members of Gwendolyn's family, including Allen, Miss Pat and Leslie. We all crowded around the conference room table. Pete began the meeting with introductions and then quickly got down to the question at hand.

In detail, he told the family of questions arising from the autopsy report and explained the need for exhumation in order to find answers to those questions. Straightforward and honest, he carefully explained to the family that the chance of a second autopsy supplying the information we needed was, in fact, remote. He then told the family that if they would like to take some time to think about it and let us know later, that would be fine.

Peering over her glasses, the diminutive Miss Pat spoke first, the strength in her voice echoing in her words. "When Clay came to my house last November, I had no hope whatsoever that it would lead to anything for Gwendolyn." She continued, setting the tone for the rest of our meeting, "But now I know God has not led us this far for us and Gwendolyn to be let down. I know in my heart that the work you all have done will find justice, and I say that if Gwendolyn needs to be taken up, then we should let her speak her truth from the grave." Each family member present spoke in support of Miss Pat's position.

Allen, his voice breaking as tears rolled down his face, was the last to speak. "My mother loved us," he stammered. "All she wanted was to see us grown up, but she was denied that. She endured a living hell. I'll never forget the way she looked that night under the house or what she said to me. For thirty-three years, I've known I was responsible for my mother's death." Allen paused to compose himself.

With a look of puzzlement, Pete asked, "Why would you say that, Allen?"

"If I had only had the courage to take Mama by the hand and pull her from under the house and run down the road for help, maybe she would still be alive," he struggled to answer. An awful silence filled the room as everyone came to grips with the magnitude of the injustice that had followed Allen for more than three decades. "I want the truth to be told for my mama once and for all," he said. "If that means she has to be exhumed, then she has to be exhumed."

Pete spoke again, "If that's what y'all wish, then I'll have the affidavits prepared to obtain a court order for exhumation, and we will proceed with the second autopsy."

On April 24, 2003, Dr. Sperry, Pete, Allen and I signed the affidavits outlining the need to exhume the body of Gwendolyn Moore and presented them to Superior Court judge Allen Keeble. Judge Keeble issued the order to exhume Gwendolyn's body.

The next step would be up to Dr. Sperry.

The Awakening

To say the next week and a half was unbearable for me does not paint the proper picture. I was now armed with a court order to exhume Gwendolyn's body. This juncture was critical; it is not every day a body is disinterred from the Hogansville Cemetery after it has been buried for thirty-three years.

Having been raised in Hogansville, I knew from experience that if someone sneezed on the east side of town, within a very few minutes, someone on the west side would say, "Bless you," and start preparing a pot of chicken soup. If word got out about the exhumation, half the town would be at the grave site when we arrived. Pete understood that this could quickly get out of hand and become a media circus that could jeopardize our case. He instructed me to set up the exhumation as quickly and, most importantly, as quietly as possible. We wanted only those on a need-to-know basis informed.

I contacted Jeff Cook, the local coroner, who is also a funeral director in LaGrange. His help proved invaluable, as he made preparations with the vault company to assist in recovering the casket from its concrete vault. In addition to executing his duties as a coroner in charge of the exhumation, Jeff would also be responsible for reburying Gwendolyn's remains. (Leslie Power actually contacted Jeff initially when seeking answers concerning Gwendolyn's death. He had directed her to the Sheriff's Department, as he, too, had suspected foul play upon inspection of old documents.)

Sheriff Donnie Turner was contacted and provided all the support and assistance at his disposal, including security at the exhumation. He assured me that both he and Chief Investigator Willis Grizzard would be at the cemetery for the exhumation; this support continued throughout the investigation.

I contacted Will Driver, superintendent of public works for the City of Hogansville, and told him of our plans, stressing the need for strict confidence until the exhumation was complete. Will met me the last week in April at the Myrtle Hill Cemetery on East Main Street in Hogansville and showed me the plot where a simple headstone stood. On it was carved "Gwendolyn M. Moore." Nothing more to tell of her life, of her being a devoted mother—just her name. The grave was on the western side of the cemetery and not totally visible from the road, which would be to our advantage. The exhumation was set for Friday, May 2. All we could do was wait.

Friday morning found me lying in bed wide awake, following a night during which my eyes had never closed. My mind never stopped turning. All I could think of was what we might—or heaven forbid, might not—find. Dr. Sperry had prepared us for the worst, and I had taken him at his word. I was physically sick with worry.

With no sleep to be had, I got up and readied myself for the day. I was the first to arrive at the cemetery that morning. Jeff Cook, Sheriff Turner, Willis Grizzard, Lynda Caldwell, David Barnes of Barnes Vault Company, Hogansville police chief Guy Spradlin and Will Driver with his crew were at the grave site by 8:00 a.m. Much to my amazement, we were the only ones at the cemetery, and our work went quickly and uninterrupted.

After a brief meeting about our plan of action and responsibilities, Will began to dig into the grave site with the backhoe. At two and a half feet, he touched the top of the concrete vault and then skillfully dug all around it while not damaging the vault itself. Will's crew climbed into the grave opening and carefully excavated all the remaining dirt from the grave by hand.

Once the crew had finished, David Barnes positioned the vault lift over the grave, and he and his team went to work with the hoist. The anticipation hung in the air as the top of the vault was removed, revealing the casket floating in the water that had collected in the vault over the many years it had lain buried. Old concrete vaults—or grave liners, as they are called—collect and hold water; newer vaults can be purchased in watertight models. David meticulously fitted lift straps around the casket and carefully lifted it into the air. Water poured from the seams of the casket, and until David was satisfied it had drained sufficiently, it remained suspended. The coffin was then lowered with precision into the rear of the

Gwendolyn's headstone. *Author's collection.*

City of Hogansville workman Will Driver (*left*) and David Barnes (*right*) of Barnes Vault Company uncovering the burial vault. *Author's collection.*

With the vault uncovered, it is ready to be opened to remove the coffin. *Author's collection.*

vault truck and thoroughly wrapped in a tarp for its journey to the crime lab in Atlanta. Throughout this procedure, there was little talk—mostly just respectful silence from the bystanders.

On the drive to Atlanta, Jeff Cook rode with me, and Lynda followed us as we trailed behind the truck carrying Gwendolyn's remains. Lyzette Strickland, the medical examiner's chief investigator, and Dr. Kris Sperry met us at the crime lab morgue. The casket was painstakingly moved from the vault truck and placed on a gurney, which was rolled into an examination room. Dr. Sperry introduced us to Dr. Rick Snow, a forensic anthropologist, who would assist him in the autopsy.

The examination room was exactly as one would imagine from images provided in movies and television shows. No windows, tiled walls and floor, steel examination tables and low-hanging fluorescent lighting. Cold. An assistant brought in tools, and the locks on the casket were opened. The only sounds heard were the clicks of the tools and the creak as the casket was opened. The lids were raised to reveal all that remained of Gwendolyn Moore. In a layer of mud-like sludge, the skeletal remains lay in the bottom of the coffin in the same anatomical position as they had for thirty-three years. The bones appeared to be coal black. I asked Dr. Sperry why they

David Barnes removing the top of the concrete vault. *Author's collection.*

Gwendolyn's remains arriving at GBI's crime laboratory. *Author's collection.*

Above: A GBI crime lab technician opening Gwendolyn's coffin. *Author's collection.*

Right: Interior of coffin; the top liner had fallen onto the remains. *Author's collection.*

were not light in color; he explained that the tannic acid created by the decomposition of grass clippings in a well-maintained cemetery filtered down into the water, which then penetrated and filled the vault. It was the dye from the tannic acid that had changed the color of the bones from light to pitch black.

The lining of the casket had long since disintegrated and fallen down in shreds to cover much of the skeleton. The cotton dress that Gwendolyn had been buried in had long since ceased to exist. Only her nylon stockings, which encased the bones of her legs, had stood the test of time.

I had both anticipated and dreaded what I was certain would be the overpowering odor of decomposition, but instead a sour, musty smell permeated the room; it was akin to the moldy confines of a damp basement. Dr. Sperry began to dictate his observations immediately. He took photographs of the interior of the casket and then stepped away to confer with Dr. Snow. Another empty gurney was placed alongside the one that held Gwendolyn's casket. Dr. Sperry explained to us that the remains would be taken from the coffin and would then be individually washed and examined before being replaced in their anatomically correct position on the adjacent gurney.

Pulling on a pair of examination gloves, he stepped next to the coffin and said, "Let's see what Mrs. Gwendolyn Moore has to tell us."

Gwendolyn Tells Her Story

ynda and I stood against the wall nearest the foot of the coffin as Dr. Sperry and Dr. Snow went to work. Close enough to see what was happening without being invasive. She and I had spoken about the anticipation of this day. Lynda was passionate about the causes she believed in, and she had dedicated herself to the search for justice for Gwendolyn Moore. I knew with her bulldogged determination, no one would be more tenacious in her pursuit than Lynda. She and I had both become so immersed in the apparent injustice of this case that I was not quite sure how either of us would handle the news if the second autopsy brought us to a premature and unjust conclusion.

Dr. Sperry lifted the skull from the mire at the bottom of the casket. It was in two pieces: the main portion of the skull and the cap, which had been removed in the first autopsy. He carefully transported the skullcap to the lab sink, where he methodically cleaned it and then examined the cap with great attention, looking for fracture lines that may have been missed by Dr. Kraftka in 1970. He spoke to us as he scrutinized the skullcap.

"There is no apparent pathology in the top of the skull," he said as he placed the skullcap on the gurney next to the casket. I felt a knot begin to form in the pit of my stomach as he cleaned the remainder of the skull. "In the absence of any soft tissue, we can only rely on the skeletal remains to give us an indication as to the cause of death," Dr. Sperry continued. "This may or may not be sufficient to render an opinion. In our case, it could prove to be a severe, if not a fatal, handicap."

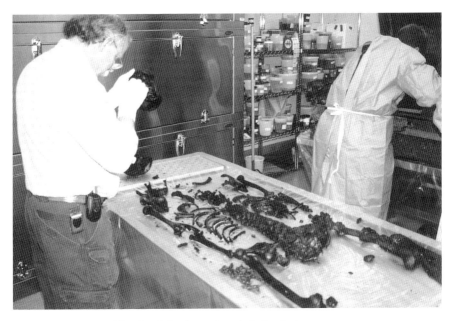

Dr. Sperry photographing the skeletal remains. *Author's collection.*

It seemed as though the good doctor was trying to prepare us for the worst. He continued to speak his findings as they emerged. "Her nose has been broken more times that I can count," he said as he examined her facial structures. "She has had a tremendous amount of facial trauma at different times as evidenced by the different degrees of healing of the nasal and facial bones. This, however, is not evidence of an injury that I can conclusively say caused her death."

As if we were a brother-sister show biz act of some kind, Lynda and I slid down the wall we had been leaning against at the same time and sat down hard on the floor in numbing silence. With a tear trailing down her cheek, Lynda sighed, "We knew it was a long shot."

Feeling defeated, I could do no more than nod in agreement, afraid that if I verbalized my reply, I, too, would be caught crying. I was completely devastated. I could not remember experiencing this type of loss since the death of my parents.

We sat next to each other, dazed and staring blankly ahead as Dr. Sperry and Dr. Snow continued to remove bones from the casket. With precision and meticulous care, they continued their work, with Dr. Sperry cleaning and reassembling the structures of the cervical spine. I remained quiet, somewhat aware of the ticking of a clock, the tinkering movement of the instruments and the steady drone of voices. As I sat with my hands over my face, attempting to maintain my composure, I heard a change to Dr. Sperry's voice. In a quizzical tone, he said, "This is provocative," as he scooped a small bony structure from the bottom of the coffin and held it up to the light.

After washing the seemingly insignificant bone clean, he examined it carefully, turning it over in his hands and then handing it to Dr. Snow, who, in turn, nodded, fully comprehending the potential importance of what he held. Dr. Sperry had once again scooped a handful of the viscous, muddy substance from the casket and was carefully washing his find. Lynda and I sat by, nervous, puzzled, anxious and intrigued all at the same time. Waiting for him to voice his thoughts was excruciating.

Finally, after moments that seemed like months, Dr. Sperry turned his attention to me and Lynda where we sat utterly defeated on the ice-cold tile floor of the autopsy room. With an eerie calm, he stated, "It's not provocative. It's murder." Our wide-eyed, stunned response begged one thing: explain! "The hyoid bone is bi-laterally fractured," Dr. Sperry said. "Mrs. Moore died of violent manual strangulation. Her life ended at the time of this injury; she was more than likely dead before she was ever placed in the well."

I couldn't believe what I was hearing. Miss Pat had been right! God had not brought us this far to let us suffer defeat. I turned to Lynda, who had elation beaming across her face. We jumped up from the cold morgue floor and

Photo of remains of Gwendolyn Moore featuring the fractured hyoid bone (circled), indicating manual strangulation as the cause of death. *Author's collection.*

simultaneously raised our hands to a jubilant high-five. Now, unabashedly, tears streamed down my face. Overjoyed, Lynda exclaimed, "We got him, Clay! We got him!"

My range of emotions was extreme. I had gone from apprehension to as low a point as I had ever experienced in my life and all the way to absolute jubilation—all within a five-minute span. It took a little while to let my nerves settle. Dr. Sperry and Dr. Snow were, by now, working in concert—steadily retrieving, cleaning and rebuilding the rest of Gwendolyn's remains.

As they were finishing their work, I asked Dr. Sperry if he was sure his finds were conclusive. Without hesitation, he stated that they were. He indicated that he would have a completed official report to us within the next few weeks. He still had to finish the examination, and he had to get the case dictated and transcribed before issuing an official report.

I was emotionally and physically exhausted on the drive back to LaGrange, but I had never felt as fulfilled professionally as I did that afternoon. I knew that we had seized a once-in-a-lifetime opportunity to right a wrong of the highest order, and with dedication and hard work, we had almost achieved what many had believed impossible. It was as if we had won the big prize.

With my eyes fixed on the interstate ahead, my mind began to wander. I could envision my daddy sitting on the tailgate of his old Ford pickup, intently listening as the hounds worked the track. In my mind, I saw Buddy, hearing that familiar bawl of his hound, turn once again with confidence to the great cast judge and, with a smile, beam, "Boss Man, you can strike my dog!"

Nearing the Journey's End

District Attorney Pete Skandalakis was thrilled with the outcome of the autopsy. Our next hurdle was to present the case to the grand jury.

Superior Court convenes with the empaneling of a new grand jury every three months, and that grand jury indicts criminal cases for that and subsequent terms. While the grand jury plays an important part in the criminal process, it is not one that involves a finding of guilt or punishment of a party. Instead, a prosecutor will work with a grand jury to decide whether to bring criminal charges or an indictment against a potential defendant—usually reserved for serious felonies. In most cases, an arrest is effected by the issuance of a warrant, a defendant is then released on bond and the case is presented to the grand jury. In some cases, however, the arrest is forgone, and the case is presented directly to the grand jury; if the grand jury presents a true bill of indictment, a defendant is formally charged with the crime and an arrest order is issued for his arrest.

The next term of the grand jury was to convene on the first Monday in August. An August indictment was my goal.

The following week, we received phone calls from the local papers regarding the exhumation. The tight security that we had been able to maintain continued to astound me. On Thursday, May 8, Lysette Strickland called to inform me that Gwendolyn was ready to be put to rest. After consulting Allen and Miss Pat, I contacted Reverend Marion Shivers in Hogansville and asked if he would provide a Christian burial. He did so eloquently, with appropriate scripture and prayer.

Lysette commented on our efforts to respectfully lay Gwendolyn to rest. "I've seen many re-interments, but never one with more dignity than this," she said. I was proud we had afforded Gwendolyn some of the dignity in death that she had been denied in life.

It was a few weeks before we heard back from the Medical Examiner's Office to let us know that the official report was available and was being posted on the crime lab website. In a less-than-confident manner, I asked if the report was consistent with the last finding Dr. Sperry had shared with us. Mrs. Bailey chuckled. "Clay, you'll just have to read it for yourself."

I opened the website with a great air of expectancy and guarded optimism. I quickly scrolled past the text of the report and, just like a kid opening his report card to get to the final grade, went directly to the last page and the conclusion. It was there I found "cause of death: manual strangulation" and "manner of death: homicide."

It was official. I called Lynda and gave her the good news. We had made the case for the murder of Gwendolyn Moore. I felt myself relax, albeit just slightly, for the first time in months.

On June 1, Lynda and Pete met to discuss the plan of action further. I expected that we would wait and present the evidence to the August term of the Troup County Grand Jury. Pete called me into his office.

"Clay, you have done a wonderful job in rebuilding this case," he said. "It's time Mrs. Moore got a little justice. We have a strong and compelling case. I see no need to wait for the grand jury to arrest Marshall Moore. Go get your warrant for malice murder and put him in jail."

I was elated! At that moment, I felt a great sense of accomplishment and felt at peace with myself. I knew in my heart that we had accomplished a task that most had felt was impossible.

Marshall Moore had hired Bill Stemberger, an attorney from Newnan, to represent him. Mr. Stemberger had accompanied Marshall when I interviewed him in April. Bill is an excellent lawyer and a decent man; Marshall made a wise choice in his selection of an attorney. No matter what the outcome, Bill Stemberger would provide him with capable and competent defense. I wouldn't have it any other way—it was time for the system to go to work and comply with the mandate of the last line of the Pledge of Allegiance, to find "justice for all."

On June 5, 2003, Marshall Moore, accompanied by his lawyer, surrendered to the Troup County Jail, where I read him his rights and placed him under arrest for the murder of Gwendolyn Moore. He was now in failing health and receiving treatment for throat cancer. Taking this into consideration, he was released on a $50,000 bond to await trial.

The Troup County Grand Jury met on August 4, 2003, at 9:00 a.m., exactly thirty-three years to the day—and minute—that I, as a fifteen-year-old boy, watched in horror as Gwendolyn's lifeless, battered body was lifted from the well. It was nothing short of mind-boggling.

Bill Stemberger initially vowed to defend Marshall vigorously at trial, but after seeing the state's case on discovery, he filed a motion to bar a trial on the grounds that Marshall had been denied a speedy trial under the Sixth Amendment of the Constitution. On September 28, 2003, a hearing was held on that motion. Lynda Caldwell argued the state's defense of the motion, and Judge Quillan Baldwin ruled that the case law was clear: the right to a speedy trial attaches at the time of the accusation, arrest or indictment, none of which had occurred until June 2, 2003. The motion was denied, and Marshall Moore was ordered to stand trial.

Based on Constitutional grounds, Marshall was entitled to appeal the denial, first to the Georgia Supreme Court and then to the U.S. Supreme Court. He was still awaiting trial. The plan for the defense in light of the overwhelming evidence had become to postpone the inevitable as long as possible.

Once again my mind played back the memories of my youth, my daddy listening intently to the change in the hound's voice as it echoed through the darkness as the chase came to an end under a towering white oak tree along the river bank. With the pride of him knowing his hound had won the hunt, he one final time turned to the ultimate judge: "Boss Man, tree my dog."

New Beginnings

The harder the conflict, the more glorious the triumph. What we obtain too cheap,
we esteem too lightly; it is dearness only that gives everything its value. I love the
man that can smile in trouble, that can gather strength from distress and grow brave
by reflection. 'Tis the business of little minds to shrink; but he whose heart is firm,
and whose conscience approves his conduct, will pursue his principles unto death.
—Thomas Paine

O ften we spend great portions of our lives in search of closure. There are some things that do not allow us emotional or mental rest until we are able to come to a definite conclusion. This phenomenon is an integral part of the human condition. How many lives have been totally devastated by an inability to move beyond the situation at hand over which those involved have no control, only to be left with the curse of having to live with the result of some terrible injustice?

Lynda Caldwell is a prosecutor who is 100 percent committed to finding that place where victims can find solace and comfort knowing that they have an untiring advocate in the search for justice. I have heard defense attorneys criticize her for her dedication to victims' rights when she remained unwavering on her recommendations on sentencing defendants. I found their criticism less a condemnation than a compliment of the highest degree to Lynda's steadfast commitment.

In January, Lynda gave me the news that her husband, Mike, had received a job offer to take the position of chief of police in Glennville, Georgia, near

Savannah, and that he was going to take the job. It was quite a blow, and I found myself becoming apprehensive at the prospect of her leaving, not just because of her familiarity with the Moore case, but because the office losing an experienced prosecutor of Lynda's caliber would be a tremendous loss.

Over the next month, Lynda searched for positions as a prosecutor in the area where Mike would now be working. In February, she was offered a job as an assistant district attorney in the Savannah Judicial Circuit, and she accepted the offer. Having a strong work ethic and stellar reputation that she did not want sullied by unfinished business, Lynda worked feverishly over the next thirty days to clear out her caseload. Her last project in our office was to write the prosecution's brief to the Georgia Supreme Court in the case of *The State v. Marshall Moore*. Her brief was superbly written—passionate, concise and based on sound case law.

The brief was presented to the state's Supreme Court on March 24, 2004. The court elected not to hear oral arguments, indicating that the case facts contained in the briefs would be sufficient information on which to base its opinion. I was confident that in order for the court to reverse Judge Baldwin's decision, it would have to set aside two hundred years of American Constitutional case law. The court would have two quarterly terms in which to render a decision; we would have our answer sometime in late 2004.

In our quest for finality and closure, we seem to forget that life is not always about the finality and cessation associated with endings. Rather, life is about finding the strength and courage to forge ahead to find new beginnings; sometimes we simply need that closure to help define the difference between the two.

We were now one more step closer to finding justice for Gwendolyn and another step closer to providing a chance for a new life to Allen, Pat and the others who had been imprisoned by the horrible injustices this case had inflicted. Lynda's devotion and ability as a prosecutor would be sorely missed as the case progressed, but now the case would fall solely into the most competent hands of Peter J. Skandalakis, who would leave no stone unturned in his own search for justice.

SOMETIMES THE TAIL SEEMS
TO WAG THE DOG

My daddy had an old southern saying for just about everything; as corny and cliché as they sometimes seemed, they were always eloquent and 100 percent appropriate. I do not even remember the circumstance, but I'll never forget any of what he said. "Son, there are times when things are just beyond your control, and in spite of your best plans and intentions, the deal gets screwed up and the tail ends up wagging the dog, and there's not a thing you can do about it." Buddy's words, as philosophical as they were at the time, I'm sure, were used to explain to me the result of some great scheme of ours that had seemed to end up going to hell on a rocket.

As comical as it sounds, no truer words had ever been spoken. Our society is, as a rule, governed by good people who try to do the right thing. For the most part, our system attempts to apply justice with kindness and compassion. The fallacy in this endeavor is when we try to apply those wonderful virtues to the members of our society who either do not have any knowledge of their meaning or are simply so callous that these virtues mean nothing to them. This absence of conscience enables those individuals to exploit these virtues as weaknesses and use them to their advantage against us. Ironically, the very traits that we hold in the highest esteem are used against our society by its enemies from within, and the tail ends up wagging the dog.

Marshall Moore had made a wise choice when he selected Bill Stemberger as his attorney. Stemberger took the case prior to Marshall's initial arrest. Moore knew that his arrest was imminent, and he cunningly retained his lawyer beforehand. Stemberger contacted the DA's Office and requested that he be contacted prior to Moore's arrest, and he would have his client surrender at the Troup County Jail. He went on to say that Marshall Moore's throat cancer had reappeared and that he would be receiving chemotherapy treatment for the condition. He then requested that Moore be allowed to receive his treatment while remaining out of confinement.

Marshall Moore had been fighting an ongoing battle with cancerous polyps in his throat and had been treated for them in the past. Treatment for this condition had affected his voice; it had become quite raspy in the last few years, but at this time, his overall physical condition appeared to be fairly stable and solid. I called Bill Stemberger and told him that we had a warrant for his client's arrest on the charge of murder.

Being the truly decent man he is, Pete Skandalakis agreed to let Moore have a bond due to the special conditions of his illness. Pete also knew that by placing Moore in jail, the taxpayers would assume a tremendous medical liability, and with the situation as it was, Moore could have actually gained financially from going to jail. Moore was arrested and released on a $35,000 bond in June 2003. At this time, Bill Stemberger proclaimed to the news media that his client was innocent of the charges and that he would seek a speedy trial and vigorously defend his innocence.

Prior to arraignment, the defense was presented with its discovery package, the disclosure of the evidence that we would present at trial. It would be this revelation that would bring about a dramatic change in the defense's philosophy. After having the chance to evaluate the case against his client, Mr. Stemberger decided that his best chance to keep Marshall Moore out of prison was to keep him out of the courthouse, and he set about to do just that. The stall was on.

After entering a plea of not guilty at arraignment, Marshall's lawyer began the tenuous high-stakes game of cat and mouse to keep his client from landing before the bar of justice. It began with his motion to bar trial, in effect asking the judge to direct a verdict for the defendant. Judge Baldwin denied the motion, but as Stemberger knew, any motion based on Constitutional grounds denied by a trial judge in a capital case goes up on automatic appeal to the Georgia Supreme Court. This move would give the defense a year before it was denied in the state's highest court. Trial was then set for the November term of the Superior Court, 2004. Stemberger then filed a motion for continuance because while Moore's cancer was in remission, an abdominal aneurysm had been found during a post-treatment CT scan.

While most aortic aneurysms I am aware of demand immediate emergency surgery, Moore was able to schedule his surgery conveniently at St. Joseph's in Atlanta on January 4, just before the beginning of the next term of court. This enabled him to move for another continuance for the February term to allow recovery time before trial. I was eager to learn how well Marshall had come through his surgery. On January 19, I called the doctor's office phone number that had been provided to us by Stemberger.

Much to my chagrin, I was informed that on the day he was to report for his pre-op exam, Marshall had come in and told the doctor that he was going to seek other treatment options for his illness. I was livid! Two terms of court had come and gone, and he had had no treatment to alleviate his malady. I ran into Pete's office ranting and raving about having been lied to and used while trying to do the decent thing. "Calm down, Clay," Pete scolded as he dialed the number to Stemberger's office. "Let's just see what he says. I can't believe he hadn't called me if Moore didn't have his surgery."

Much to Pete's dismay, Stemberger said that he had simply forgotten to call when Moore canceled his surgery. Of course, we had Moore placed on the next trial calendar, and of course, Stemberger showed up at calendar call without his client, who had now decided to have surgery in Newnan. Stemberger presented Judge Keeble with a note from Moore's doctor that basically stated that Marshall was sick and could not stand trial.

Judge Keeble glared down from the bench and placed his hand over the microphone before stating with intensity, "Damn it, Bill, I want some medical documentation from your client, not a note that a second grader would give to his teacher about why Johnny wasn't in school." Judge Keeble went on to warn Stemberger, "I don't care if he's on a stretcher. If he's not in hospital having his surgery, I expect him in court ready for trial the first trial date in March."

To no one's surprise, Moore went in for his surgery he had so desperately needed the past November just before he was to appear in court for trial in late March. Stemberger showed up again, this time to announce that his client had, in fact, had his surgery and would need six to eight weeks to convalesce before he could stand trial. There was actually some snickering in the courtroom at the announcement. Stemberger expressed outrage before the court that the genuineness of his poor client's condition would be in question. To me and to Gwendolyn's loved ones, it was the same song, second, third, fourth and fifth verse.

Every time we were denied our day in court, for days afterward, I would close my eyes at night only to see the lifeless, battered body of Gwendolyn

Moore spinning around on that cable as Allen stood to the side crying. I could hear what Moore had to say during my interview with him before his arrest: "She wasn't nothing but a sorry drunk." Bill Stemberger was correct, and I hope God will forgive me for it, but I didn't give one rat's ass about the condition of his client. I just wanted more than anything to see him stand trial for the crime he had committed so barbarically, and as much as I despised what Moore had done, I despised just as much the ones who had turned their backs on Gwendolyn and condoned her torment and murder. Just as Daddy had predicted, all I could see was the tail now wagging our dog, and it made me physically sick.

Truth Prevails

I t was my sincerest hope that Marshall Moore would live to have his day in court so that Gwendolyn could have hers. For thirty-three years, she had not felt the gentle breeze at her back or the warmth of the sun on her face. She was denied the pleasure of seeing her children grow to adulthood and the birth of her grandchildren—the simple things she would have so enjoyed in life. In death, she was denied justice by what was a corrupt and ungodly system.

In early May 2005, I received a call from one of Moore's family members who informed me that he had finally come to grips with the fact that time had run out on his bid to avoid his day in court. I was told that they thought he had made a conscious decision that he would rather die out of prison than in jail. It was for this reason that Moore had stopped eating, and his condition was in rapid decline. Moore would spend the next few weeks in and out of the hospital.

A young woman who had occasion to treat him told me that one day as he lay reading in his hospital bed, he looked at her and said in his raspy voice, "Young lady, ain't you scared of me? They call me the Boogey Man, you know." Not knowing who he was or what he was accused of, the nurse replied as she went about her business, "Why, of course not, Mr. Moore. Why would they call you that?" She said he stared ahead blankly and said without expression, "For killing my first wife." She told me at that point she finally realized who he was, and she later called me just to let me know what he had said.

I had the profound honor to be raised by a mother and father who, although not without faults of their own, imposed on me the basic principle that a man must answer for his actions. It may not be today or even tomorrow, but eventually, a day of reckoning will come. If not here, said Mama, surely in the hereafter.

Marshall Moore died on July 6, 2005, of pneumonia and malnutrition without ever having to defend himself for the murder of his wife. He may have been able to avoid his day in court on this earth, but he has since had to account for his deed to the highest of all judges, the one who knew the absolute truth. In the end, our God, a fair and just God, delivered the justice for Gwendolyn that she had been denied on this earth.

I consider it an honor to be part of a group of people who feel compelled to speak for those who cannot speak for themselves. If the time should ever come that it does not disappoint me when those voices are not heard, I'll step aside and allow someone else to pick up the gauntlet, for on that day, I will have become less than I know I should be.

If I could speak with Gwendolyn today, I would repeat the words of Jesus Christ as quoted by Dr. Martin Luther King Jr.: "The truth shall set you free." It did for Gwendolyn and for me as well. Her cries from the well were heard, and justice finally answered. Perhaps it was not the final outcome we sought, but in the end, the truth was brought to light. I feel with all my heart that Marshall Moore will eternally pay for his crime.

Gwendolyn, we heard your voice. May you finally rest in peace.

EPILOGUE

There are so many experiences with my daddy that had a tremendous bearing on the man I am today. I hope that as I go through life, I can become a much better man than I am today: a man as good, decent, forthright and justice-seeking as my father but as wise as the rock of my childhood, my mother.

The human psyche is a strange animal. Sometimes, for our own self-preservation, we need to sanitize ourselves of baggage, out of sight and out of mind. But, in Daddy's words, "It's coming up again."

The wrongs we do and the injustices we bestow on others, especially the ones that have gone undetected, we file away in a place where we keep them safely hidden from the scrutiny of others and maybe even from ourselves.

During the two years we waited for Marshall Moore to stand and be judged, I had little time to become lost in my frustration with our legal system's inability to bring him before a jury. Pete Skandalakis allowed me to reopen a seventeen-year-old missing person case that resulted in the recovery of a father's body, and hopefully that provided some closure for his children, culminating in a life sentence for his murderer in the late fall of 2004. We followed that case with one of a young man beaten and left dying on the roadside in 1990. We were able to breathe life back into a case that had languished for fourteen years. By late summer 2004, the drug dealers who had savagely beaten the young man and left him for dead over a $200 debt were sitting in jail waiting to receive a life sentence for their brutality.

During their trial, the case of a young Laotian woman who had disappeared in the fall of 1987 was brought to my attention. Her body had been found tied to a tree, where she had died of what was undoubtedly a tortured death two years after her disappearance. We would find that her tormentor had assaulted and raped others before and after the young woman's death and would continue to live among us until June 2005, when he, too, would finally find himself in a jail cell awaiting a long-overdue date with justice.

During all of these times, I could hear Mama in her last days recite her favorite verse—not for her benefit but for mine, as she knew that it would ultimately be in its simple message that I would time and again find my way: "Dear Lord, grant me the strength and serenity to accept the things I cannot change, the courage to change the things that I can, and the wisdom to know the difference."

Just as Mama knew, I would find that the wonderful philosophy of life expressed in this precious verse would allow me to find peace in most aspects of my life, especially my professional life. That is not to say that when things seem to be going badly, I don't feel the disappointment and, even to some degree, some despair. In order to be truly dedicated to this cause, I have to feel the pain of those who have been injured, I have to experience the loneliness of those who have been abandoned and I must feel the outrage of those who have been victimized. It is this that drives me to persevere for those who no longer have a voice, the Gwendolyns of this world.

About the Author

Lewis Clayton ("Clay") Bryant was born and raised in Troup County, Georgia. After high school, he began a career in law enforcement in 1973 as a radio operator with the Georgia State Patrol. In 1976, at the age of twenty-one, he became the youngest trooper on the Georgia State Patrol. While with the GSP, he attended DeKalb College and Brenau University and graduated from the Woodrow Wilson School of Law. In June 1980, after the unexpected death of his father, he became police chief of Hogansville, Georgia. He stayed in that position for twelve years until resigning in 1992 and going into the private sector, opening his own business that was later sold. In 2002, he was employed as an investigator for the District Attorney's Office in the five-county Coweta Judicial Circuit. During this time, he attended a seminar in Charleston, South Carolina, held by the NCIS (Naval Criminal Investigative Services) after solving four cold case murders, unresolved from fourteen to thirty-three years, in three years. He was recognized as the most prolific cold case investigator in the United States for single-event homicides during the time he was active in these investigations. After leaving the District Attorney's Office, he currently serves as an investigator for the Georgia Public Defender Standards Council. Bryant resides in LaGrange, Troup County, Georgia, with his wife, Beth; together they have five children: Ashley, Mary Beth, Emily, Clayton and Frank. His cases have been chronicled on *48 Hours Investigates*, *Bill Curtis's Cold Case Files* and *Discovery ID Murder Book*, as well as in a featured article in the *Atlanta Journal Constitution* and other articles in many local and regional newspapers.

Visit us at
www.historypress.com